Hereditary Diseases

Fern G. Brown

HEREDITARY
DISEASES

FRANKLIN WATTS
NEW YORK|LONDON|TORONTO|SYDNEY|1987
A FIRST BOOK

This book is dedicated to Dr. Paul M. Egel, a distinguished physician and surgeon who has used his time, effort, knowledge, and skill to help people live longer, healthier, and happier lives.

Photographs courtesy of:
The Bettmann Archive, Inc.: pp. 13, 32; Photo Researchers, Inc.: pp. 18 (Leonard Lessin), 34 and 39 (Catherine Ursillo), 42 (Robert Goldstein),53 (Omikron), 79 (NIH/Science Source); Pfizer Inc.: p. 25.

Library of Congress Cataloging in Publication Data

Brown, Fern G.
    Hereditary diseases.

    (A First book)
    Bibliography: p.
    Includes index.
    Summary: Discusses the causes, symptoms, and treatment of inheritable diseases such as cystic fibrosis, sickle cell anemia, Tay-Sachs, and diabetes and explores the field of genetic counseling.
    1. Genetic disorders—Juvenile literature.
[1. Genetic disorders. 2. Diseases] I. Title.
RB155.B67   1987   616'.042   87-8139
ISBN 0-531-10386-2
              1. Diseases - Genetic aspects.

Contents

Acknowledgments

The author and editor wish to express their appreciation to the following who have been of great assistance in the preparation of this book:

Cystic Fibrosis Foundation National Office, Rockville, Maryland: Dr. Sherry Keramidas, Susan James, medical editor, and Linda Richardson; Cystic Fibrosis Foundation, Northern Illinois Chapter.

Midwest Association for Sickle Cell Anemia: Howard Anderson, president, Dr. George Honig, Dr. Paul Heller, and Doris A. Baker, program specialist.

National Tay-Sachs and Allied Diseases Association of Chicago: Daniel M. Greenberg, Debbie Greenberg, and Kim Boyce-Hagerty.

American Diabetes Association, Inc.; Jan Lipkin; Juvenile Diabetes Foundation International; Dr. Robert J. Winter, pediatric endocrinologist, Director of Medical Education, Children's Memorial Hospital, Chicago, Illinois, and Suzanne Sanchez; Charlene Freeman, R.N., diabetes educator, Ames, Iowa and B. J. Maschak-Carey, R.N., Children's Hospital of Philadelphia.

Scoliosis Research Society: Dr. Homer C. Groves, orthopedic surgeon and Fellow of the American College of Surgeons, Evelyn Shewchuk, Jack Lipson; Ginny Lipson, and Renee Israel.

With special thanks to Dr. Mark H. Lipson, medical geneticist at Kaiser Permanente Medical Center, Sacramento, California, for his extremely helpful comments and suggestions.

Hereditary Diseases

Chapter One

WHAT IS HEREDITY?

In general, living things produce offspring like themselves. Marigold seeds grow into marigolds, and cats give birth to kittens. Human beings also produce babies that for the most part resemble their parents. How does this happen? The answer is *heredity*.

The color of your skin and eyes, whether you're tall or short, your blood type, and even your fingerprints are a result of heredity. You may be healthy or you may have been born with a hereditary disease. All of your characteristics, good and bad, were inherited through a program of genetic information your parents passed on to you. Your behavior and everything else about you is the result of your genetic program interacting with the world you grow up in. There is no other person exactly like you.

MENDEL'S WORK IN GENETICS

Gregor Johann Mendel (1822–1884) was a Catholic priest, who, because of his botanical experiments, is credited with discovering the basic laws of heredity. He was an unusual person who early in his childhood showed a love of nature and gardening and was curious about living things.

Mendel was an excellent student from a poor family, so when he was eleven years old he left home to work his way through school. When he reached college age, Mendel realized that he wasn't strong enough to both work and attend university, so, in 1843, he entered the Augustinian monastery of St. Thomas at Brünn, Austria (now Brno, Czechoslovakia) and became a monk.

He chose the monastery because it was known for its scientific activity, and it had a fine garden. Mendel hoped to pursue his botanical experiments there and prove the theory of heredity on which he was working. He believed that certain *characters* were passed from parent to offspring by a group of rules or laws. His goal was to identify the laws.

It took thirteen years, until 1856, for Gregor Mendel to get permission to continue his research. When he did, he began his experiments in the monastery garden by studying and tracing the inheritance of certain *traits* (he called them characters) of the garden pea plant. He chose this plant because it had characteristics that consistently showed clear contrast (for example, tall versus dwarf). Through his experiments he hoped to solve the mystery of human inheritance.

Mendel carefully selected the following seven traits and disregarded all others: shape of seed (smooth or wrinkled), color of first leaves (yellow or green), color of seed (light or dark), shape of the ripe pod (fat or thin), color of pod (yellow or green), position

In a nineteenth-century monastery garden, Gregor Mendel, through his experiments with the crossbreeding of sweet peas, established the basis for the science of heredity.

of flowers on the stem (top or lower), and length of stem (tall or dwarf).

First he bred several pure lines: plants that always had yellow pods, plants that always produced green ones, plants that were always tall, and so forth. When he had seven pairs of pure lines, he was ready for the next experiment.

Mendel then crossed these pairs of pure lines, mating pure tall plants with pure dwarf plants, pure green pods with pure yellow pods, and so on. He patiently awaited the results. Would some of the offspring be tall and others short, or would they be an in-between size? Would the offspring be yellow, green, or a combination of both?

From his experiments, Mendel discovered that traits are controlled by a pair of elements (which we call *genes*)—one from the mother plant and one from the father. In mating, the elements separated, and only one from each parent was passed on to the offspring. The offspring then had two elements for each trait.

In the pure tall-dwarf matings, the seeds produced only tall plants. In the pure yellow-green matings, the seeds produced only yellow plants. Mendel's experiments proved that in all of the seven contrasting traits, one in each pair was dominant over the other. Whenever it was present, it determined the trait. Mendel named the trait that showed itself *dominant*. The one that was hidden he called *recessive*.

In his next experiment, Mendel bred the offspring with one another. In this generation the recessive trait that had seemed to hide showed up again in one-fourth of the plants. There were three yellow plants and one green and so on. It proved that if a recessive element from one plant of the pair happened to combine with a similar recessive element in its mate, then its effect could appear again in the next generation.

Then Mendel crossed plants that differed in not one but two or three traits. For example, he crossed tall, smooth, yellow plants with dwarf, wrinkled, green plants. He proved his theory that the elements do not mix, but are passed separately from parent to offspring.

For eight long years, Gregor Mendel worked on his experiments and patiently recorded information on over twelve thousand pea plants. Think of the time it took to examine those thousands of plants for all seven of his selected traits and to count, sort, and keep records of each separate trait. Finally the experiments were finished, and Mendel spent another year writing the report of his findings.

In 1865, Mendel read his paper, "Experiments with Plant Hybrids," at a meeting of the local natural history society in Brünn. After all the years of observation and careful experiments he had finally solved the riddle of heredity! Although the scientists respected and liked the plump, middle-aged monk, his work was so original that they were confused by it. When read aloud, the statistical account of his many experiments was difficult to follow, and they didn't recognize the importance of his discoveries.

Mendel's paper was printed in a journal published by the society, and then sent to libraries and universities throughout Europe, but it was filed away and soon forgotten.

Years went by. Mendel was elected abbot of his monastery and was busy with his duties, but he still managed to continue his scientific experiments. He died at the age of sixty-two without knowing that future generations would call him the Father of Genetics and he would be honored throughout the world for his great contribution to science and humankind.

In 1900, sixteen years after Mendel's death, three scientists working on separate projects each thought they had discovered the basic principles of heredity. After searching the scientific literature to support their findings, they found Mendel's paper, and he was acknowledged to be the first person to propose the theories and laws of heredity. Other scientists plunged into the work. More books and papers were written on the exceptions and additions to Mendel's laws of heredity, and a new science—genetics—was born.

Although *Mendel's laws* are simplified rules of what is really a more complicated science, they are still the basis of our theories of heredity today.

REPRODUCTION

In order to understand heredity we must discuss reproduction. Reproduction is a physical process by which two individuals bring forth a new individual. The two individuals are called parents, and the new individual is the offspring. The offspring inherits genetic information from both the mother and father and as a result is usually a more varied individual. Reproduction is nature's way of assuring that our *species* will survive.

Life starts as a tiny compartment called a *cell*. The cell is a unit of protoplasm or cytoplasm surrounded by a membrane. Cells vary in size and shape, but most are so small they can't be seen without a powerful microscope. Each cell is a living unit that carries on all the functions of living matter. Our bodies consist of combinations of trillions of these cells arranged according to the rules of nature.

A human baby comes from a joining of sex cells, called *gametes*. This happens when a male *sperm* cell fertilizes an *ovum*, a female egg cell. *Fertilization* is a complicated process, but when these cells are joined they become a single new cell referred to as a *zygote*, and a baby starts growing.

A baby at conception is called an *embryo*. By the end of one month, the embryo is about a quarter of an inch (.6 cm) long and weighs much less than an ounce. After the eighth week of pregnancy, the major organ systems have been established, and the embryo is called a *fetus*. Small buds appear that will eventually grow into arms and legs. The beginnings of eyes and ears can now be seen. Between the third and fourth month the muscles start to work and the heartbeat is stronger. By the end of another month toenails and fingernails begin to develop and hair starts growing

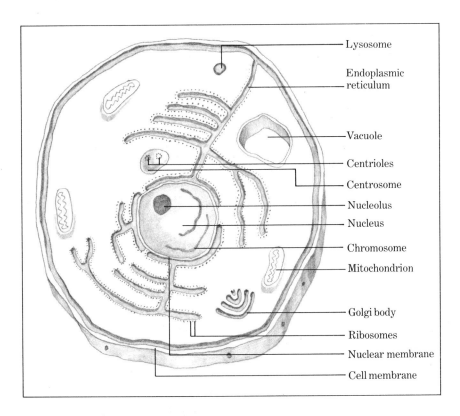

a human cell

on the head. It usually takes approximately 266 days after fertilization, about nine months, for the original zygote to multiply and grow into a baby ready to be born.

When the gametes join and become a zygote, there is a thin *membrane* surrounding the zygote. Near the center of the cell is a spherical structure surrounded by a double membrane—the *nucleus*. The nucleus controls all cell operations, and like a computer

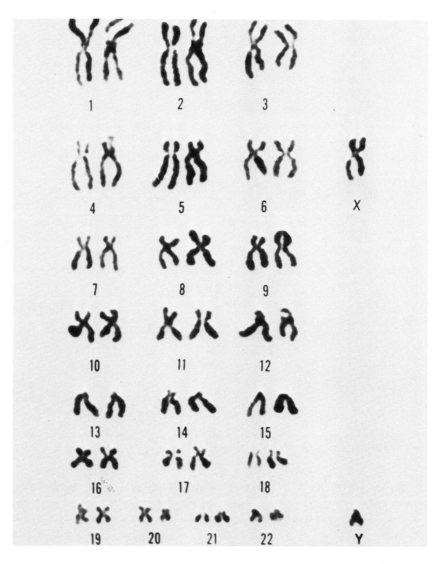

A normal male has twenty-three pairs of chromosomes.
One pair, an X and Y chromosome, determines the sex.
In a normal female, the sex-related chromosomes are XX.

it has a program of instructions that tells it what to do and when to do it. This program is the *genetic code*.

Inside the nucleus are twenty-three pairs of tiny rod-shaped structures called *chromosomes*. Where did these forty-six chromosomes come from? Half the chromosomes came from the male's sperm; the female's ovum contributed the other half. Twenty-two of the twenty-three pairs of chromosomes will appear in cells of males as well as females. They are named *autosomes*. The twenty-third pair is different in each sex, so they are called the sex chromosomes.

A baby's sex is determined by the sex chromosomes referred to as X and Y. In the female, both sex chromosomes of her pair are X, and all her ova carry an X chromosome. The pair of male sex chromosomes are not identical. Half the sperm cells carry X chromosomes and the other half Y. If one of the X sperms is first to enter the ovum, it will combine with the female's X to become XX and the baby will be a girl. If a Y sperm gets there first, the result will be XY, and the baby will be a boy. The sex of the baby is always determined by the sperm. Since both males and females are important to keep the world going, nature keeps the population of males and females fairly well balanced.

CELL DIVISION

Immediately after the zygote is formed the chromosomes move to the center of the nucleus and pull apart by pairs. Each set goes to opposite ends of the cell. A new nucleus forms around each of the two groups of chromosomes. The old cell divides and forms two identical new cells. After cell division, each new cell has a full set of forty-six chromosomes with carefully duplicated hereditary information. Because cells are living things and all living things eventually die, the cell must duplicate itself or the organism to which it belongs will also die.

Our cells keep dividing, but before they do, each cell carefully copies our hereditary information so that each of its trillions of daughter cells has its own complete set of instructions for building our whole body identical to the mother cell. This cell division is called *mitosis*.

Because cells are the "building blocks" of organic matter, they gradually assemble into other structures. Cells form into tissues. A tissue is a group of cells that carry on the same specific duties. Tissues organize into organs and glands. An organ is a group of tissues that perform similar functions. A gland is a group of tissues that carry on similar functions and also produce and secrete some type of substance.

Besides mitosis, another type of cell division occurs that we call *reduction division* or *meiosis*. Meiosis guarantees that during sexual reproduction the amount of hereditary information in the gametes is reduced by one-half. We've said that when the egg and sperm unite, the zygote receives twenty-three chromosomes from each parent. If the amount of chromosomes were not reduced, the offspring would receive forty-six chromosomes from both the father and mother and it would have a double dose of hereditary information.

What makes the cells divide and multiply? How do some cells become the nerves, blood, or skin, while others form organs of the body? How do the cells know when and how to make each part of the body?

Until the 1960s we didn't know the answers to these questions. Today, because of chemical experiments, the discovery of radioactive elements, and the invention of the *electron microscope*, where details too small to be seen with an optical microscope can be studied, scientists have been able to tell us.

GENES

On the inside, chromosomes are packed with forms called genes. They are tiny organic *molecules* that resemble beads arranged along threads. Since the chromosomes are paired, the genes are

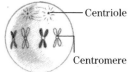
Centriole

Chromosomes

Centromere

1. The cell as it appears before meiosis. The chromosomes are not distinct.

2. The 46 chromosomes appear as distinct bodies in the nucleus. (Only 4 chromosomes are shown here).

3. The chromosomes split (double) along their length, exactly as in mitosis, held together in the center by centromeres. Meanwhile, the centriole has divided and each new centriole has started to move to opposite sides of the cell.

4. Double chromosomes that are similar line up next to each other, with some of their parts overlapping and "sticking" to each other.

5. The double chromosomes separate from each other and line up at the center of the cell. When they separate, the chromosomes take pieces of each other with them. This is called "crossing over."

6. The double chromosomes are then pulled to opposite poles of the cell. The cell begins to divide in two.

7. The original cell splits into two new cells. Each contains 23 double non-identical chromosomes. (Only 2 are shown here).

8. The double chromosomes in each cell split apart. Each half, known as a chromatid, is pulled to the side of the cell. The cells begin again to divide in two.

9. Each cell splits to form two new cells, called gametes. A gamete contains 23 chromatids. In fertilization, two gametes join to form a new cell, called a zygote, which contains the full set of 46 chromosomes.

Mitosis

— Centriole
— Nucleolus
— Nucleus
— Chromosomes

— Centromere

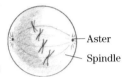

— Aster
— Spindle

1. This is a cell as it appears before mitosis begins.

2. The cell is now preparing to divide. The chromosomes become distinct bodies in the nucleus, with a split along their length, held together in the middle by the centromere. Meanwhile, the centriole divides and separates, throwing out a radiating system of protein fibers.

3. The two radiating systems formed by the splitting of the centriole are now called asters, and they travel to opposite sides of the cell. They then become connected by fibers into a system called the spindle.

4. The chromosomes arrange themselves along the equator of the spindle, midway between the two asters (centrioles).

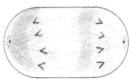

5. The chromosomes divide completely, and each set of daughter chromosomes migrates to each pole. The cell begins to divide in two.

6. The entire cell divides. Animal cells do this by pinching in two (as shown here), and plant cells do it by building a new wall.

7. Two identical daughter cells have been formed, each with the same number of chromosomes as the parent cell.

Meiosis

paired. One of each pair comes from the mother, and one from the father.

Individual genes have a certain location, or locus, on a specific chromosome. They hold the information, or *body blueprint* needed to produce *enzymes*, *hormones*, and other body chemicals for every physical characteristic a person has, such as color of skin, eyes, and hair, shape of chin and ears, blood type, and so forth.

There are millions of possible combinations of genes. It is more likely that genes on a certain chromosome will be inherited as a group, while genes on other chromosomes are apt to be inherited independently.

Each cell of a human being has up to one hundred thousand genes, and his or her own set of genes are different from those of anyone else's—except in the case of *identical twins*. Their genes are identical, but even twins have differences.

Genes copy themselves. These copies reproduce themselves into other copies and in this way characteristics are kept going for generations. If it happened that your grandfather received from his father the genes for big ears, your grandfather carried these genes as well. When he had a son—your father—he could have passed these same genes on to him. (Note: the same would hold true if the child were a girl.) Then your father could pass them on to any of his children. If you received the genes for big ears, they could be passed on to any or all of your children. This can continue generation after generation.

You've probably heard of the Morse code in which the twenty-six letters of the alphabet are encoded with two symbols—the dot and the dash. Different combinations of these dots and dashes stand for single letters of the alphabet. There is a kind of Morse code or blueprint in every single gene in our bodies that tells it exactly what each cell should do and when to do it. This versatile substance is called *deoxyribonucleic acid* (DNA). The *DNA* is the keeper of the genetic code, which is similar to the Morse code in that it sends out messages. These messages control the plan of the way people look, and determine traits such as the color of their eyes and hair and the shape of their noses or chins. But instead of using dots and dashes and forming words, as in the Morse code, the genetic code in DNA has a complex chemical makeup, and each chemical has been given a letter designation.

DNA directs the reproduction and growth of every cell in our bodies. Perhaps the instructions will tell some cells to switch off certain genes. Another time it may direct some of the cells to start a particular gene. In this way, different kinds of cells are produced for different purposes—to make body parts, to keep them working correctly, and to repair them.

Only a small part of the DNA in a particular cell is working at any one time. It is translating its instructions into materials to be used for building or maintaining the body. The rest of that cell's DNA is turned off. DNA must work only when it is supposed to at the right time and place. If it worked all the time you might find eyebrows on your toes and eyes on your feet.

You may think that if a person loses a leg due to an accident or illness the cells that remain have the blueprints needed to build a replacement leg, but they don't. The genes for building a new leg or arm are turned off long before birth, after all the organs of the body have been formed.

The rest of your hereditary information is stored in the cell, and if it divides, all your DNA will be copied exactly and passed on to the new daughter cells.

The DNA passes this information on by chemical messengers called *ribonucleic acid* (RNA). *RNA is not only the messenger,*

A model of DNA (deoxyribonucleic acid), the part of a gene that carries the code that determines individual hereditary characteristics

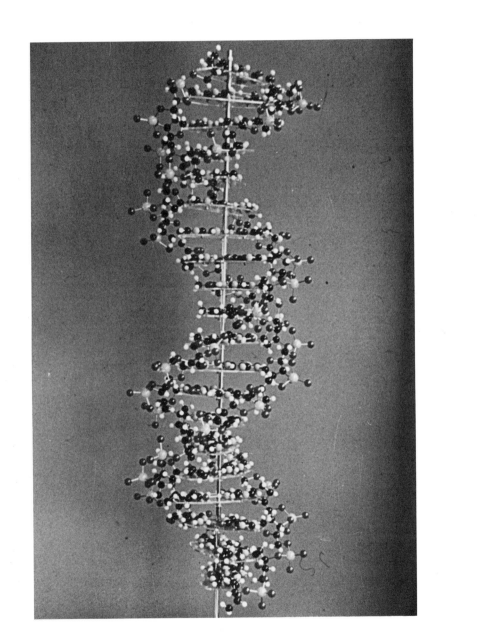

but it is also a worker that performs specialized tasks when it's told to. For example, the DNA tells the RNA the exact time to make the right material for forming eyebrows, and the RNA carries out its instructions. The DNA and the RNA work together all our lives to carry out our hereditary blueprint.

DOMINANT AND
RECESSIVE GENES

In the seven contrasting plant characters that Mendel studied, one character in each pair was dominant over the other. It is the same with humans. Our genes are also arranged in pairs, and some genes are dominant and others recessive.

A dominant gene always shows the trait whether it is paired with a like gene or not. A recessive gene, one that is hidden by the stronger gene, shows only when it is paired with another recessive gene exactly like it. As we will see in a later chapter, the recessive gene for cystic fibrosis hides until it is paired with another recessive gene for the disease. It may hide for generations.

THE EFFECT OF
ENVIRONMENT ON GENES

The genes we receive from our parents give us the potential for developing certain characteristics under the right conditions. But environment also plays a part in our heredity and affects our development. Our air quality, food, homes, schools, medical care, and the work we do are all part of our environment.

You may have inherited the genes for tallness, but your growth can be stunted if you don't get the proper nutrition and exercise. The genes for healthy skin may also have been inherited, but too much sun could cause skin cancer. Together, heredity and environment before and after birth determine our development—physically, mentally, and emotionally.

Chapter Two

WHAT CAUSES BABIES TO BE BORN WITH BIRTH DEFECTS?

When genes are changed in any way they produce permanent new characteristics we call *mutations*. Through the years, there have been mutations that have had little effect on us, while others have been important for our development. Without helpful mutations we might still be the shapeless bits of protoplasm we were a billion and a half years ago. In this book, however, we are concerned with harmful mutations that can cause serious, and sometimes fatal, disease.

It would be wonderful if everyone was born with a perfect set of chemical blueprints for building a healthy body and for keeping it that way. Yet that doesn't always happen. We know that DNA directs the reproduction and growth of every cell in the human body, and the information in the genetic code is there in a specific order. But think of how many times the cell must divide until the tiny zygote that starts a baby becomes the trillions of cells in the body of a human adult.

During cell division the cell's DNA must be copied exactly every single time the cell divides—perhaps as many as 50 billion times in our lifetime. With all the possibilities for mistakes, it's amazing how relatively few do happen. In general, human genes are only expected to mutate once in every fifty thousand to one hundred thousand times they are copied. Despite the odds, accidents do occur, and if there is a change in the genetic material, it can result in deformities and illness.

Inherited characteristics change from one generation to the next only if there is an alteration in the DNA of the sperm or egg cell. If a mutation appears in a body (somatic) cell, such as a liver or brain cell, this type of mutation cannot be passed on to the next generation, and it will disappear when the person dies.

Like any other gene, a mutated gene can be dominant or recessive or in between. Sometimes recessive mutations are hidden by dominant genes for generations before they show themselves. The mutation may be trivial—a mild blood disorder or an extra toe. It could be a cleft palate, which is fairly serious because it eventually necessitates surgery, or it might be a disease such as cystic fibrosis or Tay-Sachs which can shorten the life span.

WHAT CAUSES MUTATIONS?

Mutations are due to many complex causes. They may simply be genetic accidents, occurring for no apparent reason. Some mutations are brought about by environmental factors—exposure to radiation from the sun's rays or from radioactive material within the earth, for example. Others are caused by exposure to human-made sources of *radiation* such as *X rays* or radiation from fallout. These substances are called *mutagens*. By bringing about chemical changes in the cell, mutagens cause a breakdown in the normal structure of a gene or a group of genes.

Radiation is an extremely dangerous mutagen because a person can get a deadly dose and not feel it. The mutation that occurs may not show up until he or she becomes a parent and the genetic change is passed on to the next generation. Some mutations in sperm cells have also been related to the father's age.

TYPES OF GENETIC DEFECTS

Genetic defects occur in three different forms. There are single-gene disorders, chromosomal abnormalities, and disorders that result from the interaction of two or more abnormal genes influenced by the environment (multifactorial).

With a few exceptions, single-gene disorders usually follow Mendel's rules of inheritance. If just one of the genes is defective, life could be a nightmare if that gene is dominant. It might be a break in the DNA chain that leaves the gene unable to transcribe its message into RNA, or an extra fragment, or a chemical change in the gene.

Most defects occur on the autosomes, the twenty-two pairs of chromosomes. In this group, there are dominant and recessive disorders.

An example of an autosomal dominant disorder is *achondroplastic dwarfism*. Because of a defective change of cartilage (connective tissue) into bone, a person with this disease is considerably smaller than average and in some way is not normally formed. Every child who has achondroplastic dwarfism has an affected parent.

All children of parents with a dominant genetic defect have a 50 percent chance of receiving the chromosome with the bad gene and inheriting the disease. Have you ever drawn straws to see who should be the leader in a game? You could draw the short straw four times in a row—or perhaps not at all. It's the same for families with a dominant genetic defect. The probability of getting the disease is the same for every child in the family, whether the older children have the disease or not.

Cystic fibrosis, sickle cell anemia, and Tay-Sachs are examples of autosomal recessive disorders. For a child to have one of these diseases both parents must carry one normal gene and one recessive (nonworking) gene, and the affected child must receive one copy of the same defective gene from each parent. If only one recessive gene is present, the normal gene on the corresponding chromosome will usually turn out enough of the normal product to compensate for the defective gene, and the disease will not be passed on.

The number of genes that blood relatives, such as first cousins, have in common from their shared relatives increases the odds of combining recessive mutations in their children. With autosomal recessive disorders both males and females are equally affected.

This is not the case with *X-linked recessive inheritance*. Only males are affected by a defective gene on the X (sex) chromosomes. *Hemophilia* is an example of an X-linked recessive disease.

Remember that females inherit two X chromosomes. Their chromosomes usually provide a dominant normal gene that overpowers the recessive gene and keeps the recessive trait from showing. Females can be carriers of the disease, but the only time a female will get the disease is if she receives the mutated gene from both parents, then it will be inherited like any other recessive gene. Since this doesn't happen very often, nearly all the affected persons are males.

A male receives the X chromosome from his mother and the Y chromosome from his father. If his mother carries the recessive gene for a condition such as hemophilia on one of her X chromosomes, the boy has a 50 percent chance of receiving the chromosome with the faulty gene. If he does receive this gene, he will have the disease even though he has only one gene for it, because his Y chromosome doesn't contain the normal gene to compensate for it.

A man with hemophilia can pass the faulty gene only to his daughter, who will be a carrier without any outward symptoms

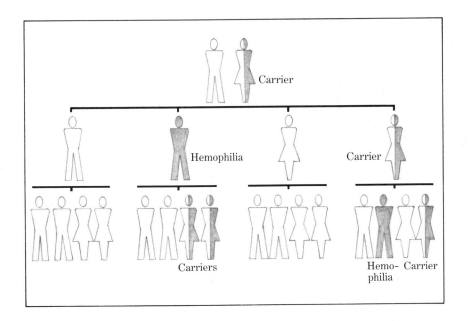

*The family tree of a hemophiliac. A peculiar char-
acteristic of hemophilia is that although women are
carriers of the gene, only men exhibit the disease.*

(unless her mother was also carrying the gene). It cannot be passed
from father to son.

Besides single-gene disorders, serious abnormalities in chromosomes can also result in genetic disease. These genetic accidents
happen during meiosis when the sex cells are forming.

One kind of error occurs in the number of chromosomes. We
know that human cells normally have forty-six chromosomes—
twenty-three pairs. We've also seen how every pair of chromosomes separates evenly as the cell divides, with each new sex cell
receiving one member from each pair. But sometimes, instead of
separating, a chromosome pair may stay together and both chro-

The most famous hemophilia carrier in history was Queen Victoria of Great Britain. Through her and her numerous female descendants, the gene for hemophilia was passed from generation to generation of European royalty.

mosomes will enter a newly formed cell. That cell will have twenty-four chromosomes. It will leave another new cell without a chromosome from that pair, and that cell will have a total of only twenty-two chromosomes. If either of these imperfect sex cells is involved in the start of a baby, the child being formed will have a chromosome number of forty-five or forty-seven. Each of these variations from the normal number of forty-six chromosomes could cause a problem. This improper chromosome separation is called *nondisjunction.*

To visualize the results of nondisjunction, think about what would happen to the sentence "The man was cold," if the letter *c* in the word *cold* was dropped and it read "The man was old." It would change the entire meaning of the sentence, wouldn't it? This is an idea of what can happen during cell division when the chromosomes do not separate properly.

If nondisjunction occurs it can cause abnormal cells that prevent the embryo from developing properly. It usually results in the prospective mother losing the baby early in pregnancy, sometimes even before she knows she is pregnant. Despite the fact that miscarriage usually occurs when there are abnormal numbers of chromosomes, sometimes children with this defect do survive. The most common condition of this kind is *Down's syndrome,* which is also called *trisomy-21* because those with the disease have three(tri) of chromosome twenty-one, instead of a pair.

Nondisjunction can occur in the egg or sperm to couples of any age, however the chances of it happening are greater in older women during the first division of the egg cell. Defects caused by chromosomal abnormalities are much higher when the prospective mother is over thirty-five, and increase in frequency as a woman gets older.

There is another type of accident that can occur when sex cells are being formed. As the DNA is reproducing, a tiny piece of a chromosome may be lost, or a part of one chromosome may break off and become attached to another chromosome. The abnormality that occurs is called *translocation.*

A Down's syndrome child, the result of improper chromosome separation, in which the cell contains three of chromosome twenty-one, instead of a pair

When the cell divides again after translocation, two things can happen. The chromosome that lost the piece and the chromosome to which the extra piece was attached might just go to the same sex cell. This is called a balanced translocation, and if that sex cell helps form a baby it may not affect that person. All the needed genes are there in the right amounts, even though they are not all attached to the right chromosomes.

It could be something like this sentence where the misplaced letter doesn't make much difference: "Th man was colde." We are able to figure out the sentence without losing the meaning. It's where the change occurs that is important.

A balanced translocation may have no visible effect on a person but it could cause trouble when he or she has children. During cell division the sex cells could produce sperm or eggs with a badly unbalanced set of chromosomes.

Besides the mother's age, heredity, too, can play a part. Some families have more trisomies than others, and a woman who has already given birth to a Down syndrome child is at higher-than-normal risk of having another.

There are also diseases that result from at least two inherited abnormal genes interacting with environmental factors. This is called *multifactorial inheritance*. Such disorders seem complicated because they don't follow Mendel's laws of inheritance, and some don't appear until later in life. Recent studies point out that these diseases seem to run in families, but researchers haven't yet found how they are inherited. These types of birth defects include congenital heart defects, cleft palate, hip dislocation, cleft lip, and spina bifida.

Chapter Three

GENETIC COUNSELING

A genetic counselor is a trained medical specialist who uses modern medical technology to fight birth defects, and can predict what the percentages are that a couple will produce a child with a genetic disorder. A counselor also helps families whose children have a genetic disease cope with their problems.

When Marc and Susan Haver were told that their child had been born with cystic fibrosis, they were so shocked and angry that they tried to deny it. The entire family went through a terrible period of grief. They had expected a normal, healthy, fat-cheeked baby like the ones in the TV ads, but Marc Junior had inherited a disease so serious that it could shorten his life.

In the case of Todd and Rebecca Gold, their baby daughter, who had been developing normally for six months, had begun to lose her coordination and now she could barely hold up her head. When the doctor told them that she had *Tay-Sachs* they were so upset that the illness put a tremendous strain on their marriage.

Both families turned to their doctors for help and were referred to a medical genetics clinic for genetic counseling.

Nancy and Brian Hughes had been married for four years. They wanted to become parents, but they were afraid to have children because Brian was a *carrier* of sickle cell disease. They needed to know what the chances were of their child being born with the disease. They made an appointment with a genetic counselor.

Rachel Warren was pregnant and she was worried about her baby's health because she already had a child with Tay-Sachs disease. There was a 25 percent chance that another child would have the disease, and she wanted to know if the child she was carrying was normal. She went to a genetic counselor to find out.

WHO NEEDS
GENETIC COUNSELING?

When there is a history of an inherited disorder, a birth defect, or mental retardation in a family, it's suggested that prospective parents consult a genetic counselor before having children. If the prospective mother is thirty-five or older, or the parents are from an ethnic background that tends to have a high rate of genetic abnormality—such as sickle cell disease in blacks, or Tay-Sachs in Eastern European Jews—genetic screening is advised.

Prospective parents may want to consult a genetic counselor if one or both have had long-term exposure to substances such as radioactive material, pesticides, or anesthetic gases which may harm the baby. If the mother-to-be has a problem getting pregnant, or has had several miscarriages, early infant deaths, or both, genetic counseling may help to find out what's wrong.

HOW DOES GENETIC
COUNSELING WORK?

When a family who is at risk or already has a genetic disorder comes from counseling, the first step is usually for the geneticist to go over the medical facts of the particular disease in simple language, discussing the diagnosis, treatment, and what can be expected in the future. The counselor will then explain how heredity works, and the risks involved to others in the family.

Genetic counselors also inform and help couples make important decisions about becoming parents. After gathering all the pertinent family history, applying the laws of heredity to this information, and studying the results of various diagnostic tests, the counselor is usually able to predict the chances of a child being born with a defect. Prospective parents can then decide whether or not to have a child. Counselors do not make the decisions, but they help couples weigh the consequences of their decision, often working in teams to answer all the questions that are asked.

Psychological support for families like the Havers, Golds, Hugheses, and Warrens (who already have a child with a hereditary disease) is another aim of genetic counselors. They are well aware of the everyday stress patients and parents go through, and they try to get families to talk about their feelings. This is valuable for the patient and the family because it helps them feel better about themselves, which is as important as knowing all the medical facts about the disease.

If the family wishes, the counselor can put them in touch with others who have the same disorder. Counselors also inform patients about community resources and agencies available to help them deal with their particular problem.

As for Rachel Warren's anxiety about the health of the baby she was carrying, if she had asked the question, Is my baby normal? before the 1950s, nobody could have given her an answer until the baby was born. Today the genetic counselor can ease Rachel's mind. By performing certain tests and evaluations Rachel will get her answer. It is now possible to diagnose a number of gene and chromosome disorders before a child is born.

DETECTING
GENETIC DISORDERS

Genetic counseling relies on the pedigree, or family tree, for information about diseases, deformities, and deaths. Pedigree analysis

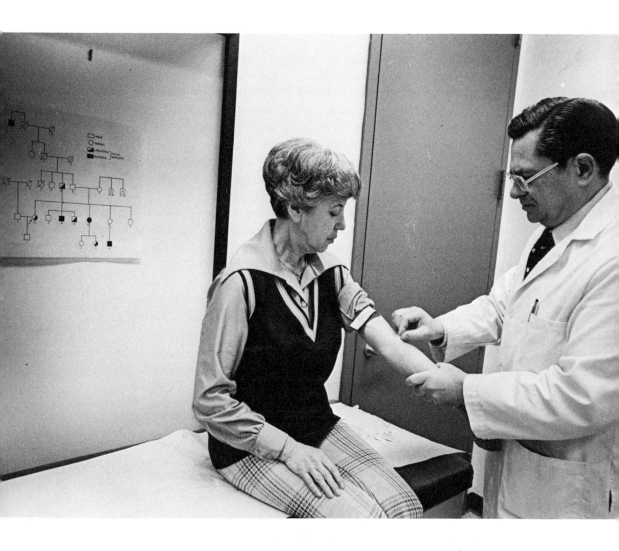

Genetic counseling is advised for a prospective mother over the age of thirty-five. Through diagnostic tests and the gathering of pertinent family history, the genetic counselor can make a determination as to the chances of a child being born with a defect.

is the study of a trait or disease in the patient's family to help determine how it is inherited and how often it might occur.

The first step for Rachel Warren's counselor was to take a complete family history, asking questions about relatives in the last few generations who have had the disease. This information was considered along with the doctor's report and then a decision was made as to which laboratory tests were to be given.

Most screening tests for Tay-Sachs are simple, relatively safe, and fairly inexpensive for identifying carriers of defective genes and hence babies at risk because of the disease.

The doctor might study both prospective parents' chromosomes taken from the cells of the blood, skin, or from the amniotic fluid (a *karyotype*). Chromosome studies can also be done on a child with multiple birth defects and mental retardation to look for chromosomal abnormalities.

Cells from each sample are grown in a special culture until chromosomes can be seen with a microscope. After staining, the cells are examined for abnormalities.

Rachel Warren was a special case. She was in the high-risk category because she was already pregnant and had one child with a genetic disease. Since she wanted to know if the child she was carrying was normal, her counselor suggested she have *amniocentesis*.

TOOLS OF
THE GENETIC
COUNSELOR

Amniocentesis is usually done in the sixteenth to eighteenth week of pregnancy. It gives the doctor and the counselor an early clue to what is happening with the unborn child. Through this procedure some illnesses and deformities in the fetus can be diagnosed. Amniocentesis can show many chromosomal abnormalities and well over one hundred inherited biochemical disorders. Although amniocentesis routinely tests for chromosomal abnormalities, no other tests are performed on the fluid unless a couple is at risk, for example, for a metabolic disease.

What is amniocentesis?

Before a baby is born, it grows inside its mother suspended in a fluid-filled bag that keeps it warm and safe. This bag of tissue is called the *amnion*. The fluid that surrounds the fetus, and resembles urine, is the amniotic fluid. It contains water, dissolved salts, chemicals, various waste products, and discarded cells from the fetus.

For amniocentesis, a doctor carefully inserts a long, hollow needle through the mother's abdominal wall into the amniotic cavity, and a small sample of amniotic fluid is drawn out. The cells sloughed off from the fetus are grown in a culture and studied.

In Rachel Warren's case, there was good news. Her baby was healthy. If the baby hadn't been normal, the Warrens would have been told of the options open to them. They could have chosen abortion or prepared for the birth of the child knowing it would have a genetic disorder.

In some cases, prompt treatment before the baby is born, or right after, can minimize the symptoms of a genetic disease and help the child develop relatively normally. A doctor recently reported a case where, through amniocentesis, a genetic defect was found in an unborn baby. The expectant mother was given a vitamin B_{12} supplement to combat the defect. The vitamin passed into the baby's blood and the child was born healthy.

Amniocentesis is also used for women over thirty-five who, because of their age, have a greater-than-average chance of having a child with chromosomal abnormalities.

Although many genetic diseases can be detected before birth by amniocentesis, and it is considered by geneticists to be a valuable tool, there is some risk in using it. Amniocentesis has been known to cause bleeding, infection, or miscarriage, so it must be performed with care by a skilled doctor.

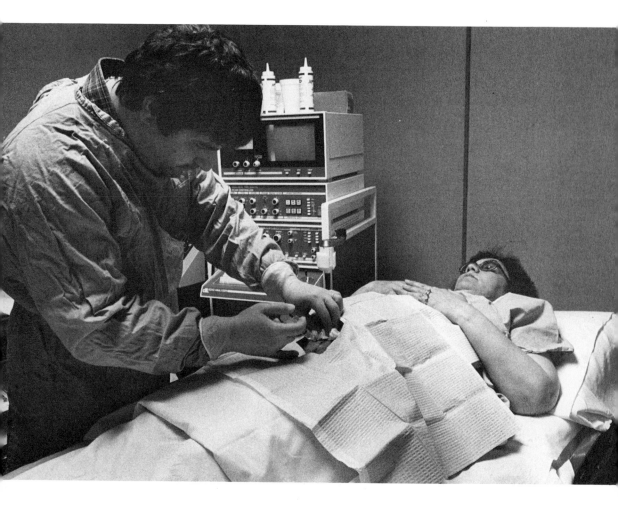

In amniocentesis, the doctor withdraws a sample of
amniotic fluid, which contains cells from the fetus.
These cells are then grown in a culture and studied to
determine the sex of the baby and whether there are any
abnormalities. The ultrasound scanner shown in the
background of the photo is used to locate the best spot in
which to insert the needle so as not to disturb the fetus.

Ultrasound is an important tool that genetic counselors use apart from amniocentesis and also before amniocentesis to make sure the needle is inserted in a safe spot. It is also prescribed when additional information about the fetus is needed to counsel patients. Ultrasound works like the underwater detection devices submarines use. A sonic beam passes through the pregnant woman's amniotic fluid and via electronics an amazingly clear picture is produced providing the doctor with information as to the state of the fetus. With these tools, doctors can accurately date the pregnancy and diagnose fetal problems.

A new method to diagnose genetic disease, called *chorionic villi sampling*, is being tested. This can be done in the ninth to eleventh weeks of pregnancy, at least seven weeks earlier than amniocentesis. It is relatively painless. A catheter guided by ultrasound is inserted into the uterus to withdraw a small amount of chorionic villi tissue. The sample is not part of the fetus, but it contains fetal tissue, and can be analyzed.

The chorionic villi are protrusions on the chorion membrane, which surrounds the fetus and later becomes the placenta. Results are available much sooner with this test than with amniocentesis. If chorionic villi testing proves to be safe and accurate, it may eventually replace amniocentesis.

VALUE OF GENETIC COUNSELING

Until recently, it was difficult to find a competent genetic counselor in the United States. Today we have many genetic laboratories and qualified counselors who perform diagnostic tests for all kinds of genetic disorders. With ongoing research, more and more genetic conditions are becoming treatable.

Besides testing, advising, and answering questions, genetic counselors give psychological support and reassurance to patients and their families. This support is extremely valuable to people who must deal with hereditary diseases and disorders.

Chapter Four

CYSTIC FIBROSIS

It was a hot day when Susan Haver brought four-month-old Marc Junior to the doctor. The baby was cranky and out of sorts. Mrs. Haver was worried because her son had a severe wheeze and cough. She feared that he had bronchitis. She also told the doctor that although Marc Junior ate well, he seemed to be thin and undernourished, and his stools had an exceptionally bad odor and a bulky look.

The doctor examined the baby and, taking into consideration what Mrs. Haver had told him, ordered several laboratory tests and a chest X ray.

One test showed that there was a high salt content in the baby's sweat—a symptom of cystic fibrosis (CF) found in nearly all patients. The excessive salt that Marc Junior's body excreted, along with the thick mucus his body produced, confirmed the *diagnosis* of cystic fibrosis. The disease was not detected earlier because the baby's lung and digestive disorders seemed to be symptoms of other childhood diseases, such as allergies. But quick diagnosis and treatment may now prolong Marc Junior's life.

CF is the number one fatal inherited disease among young people in the United States. It primarily affects the lungs and digestive system. Approximately one baby in every two thousand is born with CF. It occurs in males and females alike, mainly among whites.

In most people, mucus is thin and slippery, and it helps to clean the dust and germs from the lungs and breathing passages. The body of a person with CF produces abnormal amounts of thick, sticky mucus that tends to clog the air passages in the lungs and interfere with breathing. Mucus may also block the ducts of the *pancreas* (the irregularly shaped gland behind the stomach), preventing digestive juices from reaching the intestines. As a result, food passes through the body without being broken down and absorbed, and the patient doesn't get proper nourishment.

Since CF is a genetic disease, it is always present at birth, but it may not develop for months or even years later. Some of the symptoms are common to nearly all patients. Others with CF have fewer symptoms of the disease. This puzzles researchers who wonder why people are affected differently.

WHAT ARE THE SYMPTOMS OF CYSTIC FIBROSIS?

Generally there are three major symptoms of this disease: respiratory problems; digestive problems, which occur in 85 percent of the patients; and high amounts of salt in the sweat.

Most CF patients develop lung disease at some time in their lives. The thick mucus produced in CF clogs the airways of the lung and respiratory system, interfering with normal breathing, and harboring infections which eventually damage lung tissue. Respiratory complications are the main cause of death of patients with CF. These patients are also susceptible to lung infections that are resistant to certain kinds of antibiotics.

The pancreas and other organs of the digestive system secrete enzymes into the intestine where they help to break down food into elements that the body needs for energy, growth, and maintenance. In CF, thick, sticky mucus blocks the passageways that carry these enzymes to the intestine. This causes problems with digestion, and the food that is not broken down cannot be used by the body, so it is excreted. Marc Junior ate well, but because of his bowel problem, he seemed to be malnourished.

CF affects the sweat glands so that there is a large amount of salt in the perspiration of CF patients, especially when sweating is increased as during exercise, in hot weather, or with a fever. The excessive salt loss can cause heat exhaustion or dehydration—loss of water from the body.

HOW IS CYSTIC FIBROSIS TRANSMITTED?

CF is not contagious. It is a hereditary disease caused by a defective or abnormal gene on one of the twenty-three pairs of chromosomes.

It is estimated that one in every twenty Americans is a carrier of this defective gene. Inheriting a single gene for CF doesn't cause a problem, though, and often people don't even know they are carriers until they become parents of a CF child.

The child with cystic fibrosis has inherited a pair of recessive CF genes. One gene from the pair is from the father and one from the mother. Just because both parents are carriers, it doesn't mean that all their children will have CF. There is a 25 percent chance with each pregnancy that their child will be normal, a 50 percent chance that their child will be a carrier, and a 25 percent chance that their child will have the disease. So this means that there is a 75 percent chance that their child will not have CF. The chances are the same for each pregnancy, even if there is a child in the family who already has CF.

Although we know how one gets CF, we aren't exactly sure where in our DNA the gene that causes it is located. Let's suppose there is a protein in the body whose role it is to thin out mucus, among other things. If the gene for that protein is abnormal, as it is in CF patients, then the protein would come out wrong and be unable to perform its function.

Researchers still don't know which of the body's one hundred thousand genes is the CF gene or which protein is abnormal. Due to a recent scientific discovery, however, we now know that the CF gene is somewhere on the long arm of chromosome seven, and that this gene is present in every cell of a person with cystic fibrosis.

So the search for the abnormal gene has narrowed. Scientists also have the advantage of using the information they already have about chromosome seven as they work to identify the CF gene.

WHAT IS THE TREATMENT
FOR CYSTIC FIBROSIS?

Although researchers are getting closer to finding the gene responsible for CF, other options are being explored, too. But until a cure for cystic fibrosis is found, the aim of treatment is to help the person with CF live as normal a life as possible. And to offset additional problems, it's important for patients and family to know all about the disease and how it is treated.

Because the disease affects each patient in a different way, individual treatment is necessary. Treatment generally includes bronchial drainage (postural drainage), a form of chest physical therapy that helps loosen mucus from the lungs and keep lung passages open; antibiotic therapy, drugs that help fight respiratory infections; and dietary management.

To combat pancreatic enzyme deficiencies, the treatment includes oral pancreatic enzymes with meals and snacks. This replaces enzymes blocked in the pancreatic ducts. Children with CF generally need to eat more because their bodies require more energy.

Other dietary measures include generous salting of foods, and salt supplements in hot weather to combat sweat loss. For many years, CF patients were told to limit fats in their diet, but today's thinking is that with the proper amounts of pancreatic enzyme replacements, most CF individuals don't have to be on fat-restricted diets. A balanced, highly nutritious diet is very important, however, and generally vitamin supplements are prescribed.

Some CF patients take as many as forty to sixty pills a day. The individual cost of CF treatment and care can range from six thousand dollars to twelve thousand dollars per year, and sometimes higher if there are complications that require frequent hospitalizations.

WHAT'S IN THE FUTURE
FOR CF PATIENTS?

When the Cystic Fibrosis Foundation was established in 1955, few CF children lived beyond five years of age. Today, nearly half those children born with CF can expect to live into their twenties and even beyond.

At thirty-one years of age, Jim Kerwin has beaten the odds and lived longer than most CF victims. He is married and works full time at a management position in a manufacturing firm.

Jim has probably lived this long because he has a relatively mild case of CF. He says he has hope for the future because researchers are working hard to find new treatments for him and the thirty thousand other young Americans who have cystic fibrosis.

Although Jim is managing well for a person with CF, his life is not easy. He often has to go into the hospital for what he calls "tune-ups." These treatments include large doses of antibiotics, and he is pumped full of calories to replace the weight he has lost. He also receives postural drainage where his body is tipped at a 35-degree angle and his chest is clapped to drain the mucus.

When Jim is feeling good, he doesn't stay on any special diet, but he stays away from too many dairy products and takes heavy doses of vitamin C. He likes to swim, run, and ride his bicycle. But his favorite physical activity is medium weight lifting with lots of repetition, and he makes sure that he inhales and exhales deeply when exerting this force. Jim says, "I feel that deep breathing is very beneficial to me."

Jim is one of the lucky ones. He is working and married. He is unable to father children, though—because like most CF males, Jim is sterile.

Research now in progress has made this the best of times for cystic fibrosis patients. By some estimates, the CF gene may be found within a year or two. Other researchers say it won't be quite that soon, but everyone agrees that identification of the gene will be here before long.

When this happens, scientists will be able to study the gene and its product and develop new treatments.

Another possibility for treating CF is through drugs. When it is determined which protein is abnormal or lacking in the CF patient, it can be manufactured and then given to the proper organs at the right times. However this treatment has its problems. Let's say we have the protein that breaks up the sticky mucus in the pancreas; how do we get it to the pancreas? Doctors would have to work out some way.

Researchers are also working at formulating safe, effective tests for detecting the CF gene. Although such a test may take a long while to develop and could be expensive, when it is finally made available it will help doctors identify carriers of CF who have no outward symptoms of the disease. It could also be used to tell a pregnant woman who has already had a CF child whether her developing baby is affected as well.

While geneticists are working to find the CF gene, physiologists and cell biologists are studying cells in the lungs and sweat ducts to investigate what has gone wrong in cells affected by CF. Cellular research has already shown that in CF patients, a certain substance, namely chloride, does not move in and out of the cells properly. This could possibly lead to the salty sweat and the sticky mucus in individuals with CF.

When biologists understand what is wrong with the cell, it will help geneticists who are studying the gene find what is wrong with the gene's message to the cell. Then they can identify the gene, not only by location but by what the gene does.

Identifying the CF gene will not mean that scientists have found a cure for the disease. But it will help them to continue working to pinpoint the gene's exact defect. When they find it, doctors will be able to develop new and better treatments for Marc Haver, Jr., Jim Kerwin, and other people with cystic fibrosis.

Chapter Five

SICKLE CELL ANEMIA

When Janey Adams was six months old, it seemed to her mother that Janey's hands and feet were swollen, and she cried as if she were in pain. Mrs. Adams took the baby to the doctor for a checkup.

The doctor examined Janey and found that besides the symptoms her mother had noticed, she had a yellowish tinge on the whites of her eyes which could be a symptom of a blood disorder. He ordered a blood test. The results showed that Janey had sickle cell disease.

With proper diet, rest, and exercise, Janey managed the disease very well for a number of years. When she was five years old, Janey was small for her age. "You'd think she was a three-year-old," said her mother, "and she's about to go to school." Although Janey was extremely excited to be a kindergartner, when the day finally came, she was doubled over with a bad stomach ache. Mrs. Adams took her temperature and found she had a low-grade fever. Janey had to stay home. As the day went on, her pains got worse, and Mrs. Adams noticed that Janey's urine was quite dark.

The doctor said it was a sickle cell crisis—Janey's first. He told Mrs. Adams that Janey would have these attacks every once in a while. The crisis may have been caused by the excitement of going to school, or being overtired—they didn't exactly know what had brought it on. But Janey was a very sick little girl. For over a week, Mrs. Adams kept her in bed and gave her a lot of fluids and medication prescribed by the doctor to ease the pain.

When she was better, Janey was able to go to school. The teacher was told of Janey's illness, and she was careful to see that Janey rested after recess and physical activity.

Now that Janey is eight, she knows what she can and cannot do. When she feels well, she can run, jump, and climb the way the other children do. Janey can't let herself get too tired, though, and she must try not to catch cold. She has been hospitalized a few times in the last three years, but now she takes it in stride when she has to go into the hospital.

WHAT IS SICKLE CELL ANEMIA?

Sickle cell anemia is an inherited disorder of red blood cells that results from a defective *hemoglobin* molecule, called hemoglobin S. Hemoglobin is a protein found in the blood cells. Healthy red blood cells are shaped like a doughnut. The red color comes from millions of hemoglobin molecules in each cell. Hemoglobin carries oxygen from the lungs to all parts of the body.

When a normal red blood cell releases its oxygen, it remains doughnut-shaped. If cells contain sickle hemoglobin, once the hemoglobin releases its oxygen the cells become rigid and rough. When this happens, they elongate and change from their normal doughnut shape to a sickle shape (like the farmer's tool with the semicircular blade). This is called sickling.

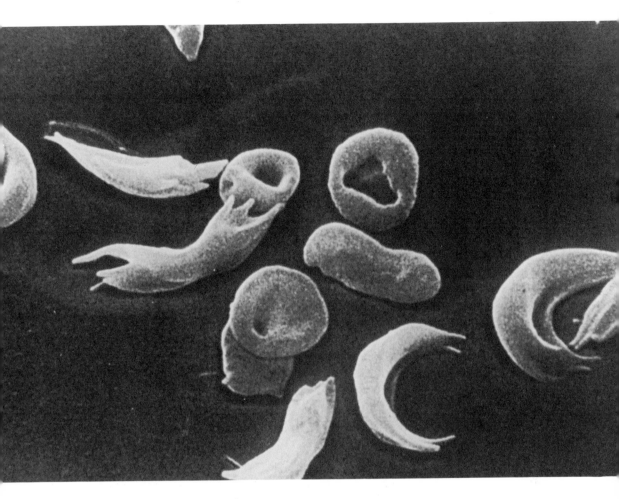

*A scanning electron micrograph (SEM) of the red
blood cells of a person with sickle cell anemia.
In this disease, when the red blood cell releases
its oxygen, instead of remaining doughnut-shaped,
it elongates and assumes a sickle shape.*

Although sickle hemoglobin carries as much oxygen as normal hemoglobin, there are important differences. Normal cells are soft, like a bag of gelatin, so they can change shape and easily flow through small blood vessels. But sickle cells are hard, like pieces of stone, and often jam up in small blood vessels. This stops the blood from flowing.

Normal, doughnut-shaped cells live about 120 days. Sickle cells live less than half that time. New red blood cells cannot be made fast enough by the body to replace the sickle cells that are being broken down, so the body has fewer red cells and less hemoglobin than normal. This produces a condition called anemia.

Individuals with sickle cell anemia endure severe pain crises, caused by the blocking of the blood vessels with sickle cells, or the anemia. Sickle cell disease can lead to a stroke and other complications, and may leave its victims susceptible to infections and disease—even premature death.

WHAT ARE THE SYMPTOMS OF SICKLE CELL DISEASE?

The makeup and severity of sickle cell disease differs in various age groups. Some people never become seriously ill. Others may have only some of the signs and symptoms of the disease, and still others will have many of the symptoms.

Sickling usually begins in one part of the body, like the joints of the leg or the stomach, but it can occur anywhere at any time. In people with sickle cell disease, tissues are starved for oxygen, and it results in pain that can last for hours—even weeks. These sickle cell crises may happen several times a year.

Some of the common symptoms are tiredness and sores on the leg, particularly around the ankle, that are slow to heal. Because the small blood vessels are plugged up, the hands and feet may swell and get hot and painful. Children with sickle cell disease may be below average size, and they can be susceptible to respiratory infections.

HOW IS SICKLE CELL
ANEMIA TRANSMITTED?

Sickle cell anemia is not contagious. You can't catch it from a friend or get it from a blood transfusion—you're born with it. We know that chromosomes are composed mostly of DNA which provides the blueprint for our development, and that mutations are changes in the DNA blueprint, or gene. Sickle cell disease began as a mutation.

The exact origin is unknown, but it is thought that the first mutation happened over one thousand years ago in western, northern, and central Africa. It was presumably passed on from generation to generation until the present. There are approximately fifty thousand victims of sickle cell anemia in the United States. The disease is more common in blacks, but it occurs in people of Greek, Spanish, Turkish, Italian, Asiatic, and Indian descent as well, and in others who come from the Mediterranean area.

It's possible that the hemoglobin S–producing gene has survived throughout the years because it has helped protect people against malaria, a serious disease common in hot climates.

Since sickle cell disease is hereditary and caused by an abnormal or recessive gene, a pair of these genes must be present for the person to have the disease.

All people inherit two genes for hemoglobin, one from each parent. Suppose gene N is normal hemoglobin, and gene S is the faulty gene for sickle cell hemoglobin. Mr. and Mrs. Adams each had one N gene and one S gene. If Janey had inherited from her parents two hemoglobin genes that were N, she would have had normal blood. But Janey inherited two genes that were S, and she got the disease.

SICKLE CELL TRAIT

Everyone who has sickle hemoglobin in their red blood cells does not have sickle cell anemia. Some are just carriers of the gene and their condition is called sickle cell trait. One out of ten black Americans has sickle cell trait.

Janey's parents had no symptoms of the disease, but they both had sickle cell trait. Because their first two children were healthy, it was a shock for them to find that they had passed the sickle cell disease on to Janey.

The genetic counselor explained to the Adamses that one of the major differences between sickle cell anemia and sickle cell trait is that whenever a drop of blood is taken from a person with sickle cell disease and examined under a microscope, some sickle cells can be seen. In a drop of blood from a person with sickle cell trait the cells always look normal (doughnut-shaped). But after they are out of the body, if oxygen is removed from the cells, they can be made to sickle. The reason for this is that practically all the hemoglobin in cells from those with sickle cell anemia is sickle hemoglobin, whereas in the person with sickle cell trait only about half is sickle hemoglobin, the other half is normal.

Because there is no sickle-shaped hemoglobin in their blood, those with sickle cell trait do not have anemia, pain, or any of the symptoms of sickle cell anemia. Under certain conditions of severe oxygen reduction, however, such as might happen if the person is flying in a small, nonpressurized airplane above 8,000 feet (2 km), sickling could occur because the air inside the plane is just as thin (less oxygen) as the outside air.

The Adamses' counselor further explained that with each pregnancy, Mrs. Adams had a 25 percent chance that the child would have sickle cell disease, a 50 percent chance that the child would have sickle cell trait, and a 25 percent chance that the child would have normal hemoglobin.

Janey's brother and sister were given a simple blood test to see if they had sickle cell trait, but the results were negative. It was just a matter of chance that Janey had the disease while the other two children were completely disease-free. In the event that Mrs. Adams were to have another child, the same odds would hold true.

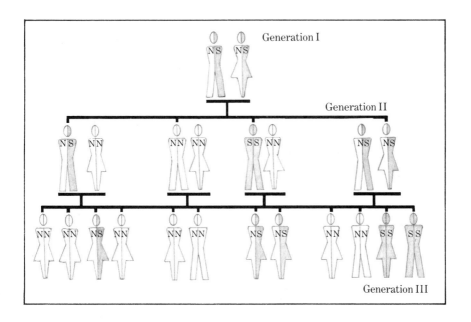

The inheritance of sickle cell anemia. This family tree shows some examples of the inheritance of sickle hemoglobin. In the first generation, each parent has one gene for normal (N) hemoglobin, and one gene for sickle (S) hemoglobin. Both parents are therefore carriers—they have sickle cell trait. Since the father is NS, he has sperm with either N or S genes in about equal numbers. The mother is also NS; she has both N and S eggs in about equal numbers. Thus it is equally probable that a sperm carrying a hemoglobin N gene or a sperm carrying a hemoglobin S gene will unite with an egg carrying a hemoglobin S gene.

In the generations that follow, a child who receives one S gene from a parent and one N gene from the other parent will have sickle cell trait. The child who receives one S gene from one parent and one S from the other parent will have sickle cell anemia. And the child who receives one N gene from one parent and one N gene from the other parent will have normal hemoglobin, and will not be a carrier.

If Mrs. Adams were pregnant now, a prenatal diagnosis could be made by taking a sample of fetal blood or amniotic fluid. But when Janey was born, the Adams family weren't aware that she had the disease, because she wasn't tested at birth. Her symptoms didn't show until she was six months old.

Although the hemoglobin in the blood of a person with sickle cell trait is different from most people's, that person can expect a normal life span. Sickle cell trait never progresses to sickle cell disease. Those with sickle cell trait sometimes notice blood in their urine. It's not serious, but should be reported to the doctor.

If a couple both have sickle cell anemia, they must carefully consider the risks of becoming parents. Childbearing is dangerous for a woman with the disorder, and all the offspring will have sickle cell disease. If one parent has sickle cell anemia and the other has normal hemoglobin, all their offspring will be carriers of the sickle cell trait.

TREATMENT

There is no cure yet for sickle cell anemia; we can only relieve the symptoms. Victims of the disease are taught to eat properly, get enough rest, and exercise moderately. They can usually do most things that others their age do, if it isn't too strenuous.

When a sickle cell crisis does occur, the patient is usually treated at home. Some patients are put to bed, given plenty of fluids, and medication for pain. If pain persists, a doctor should be called. When there is an infection, antibiotics are often prescribed.

There are many possible complications of sickle cell disease. Treatment ranges from medical to surgical and will vary with the complication. Sometimes the patient's hemoglobin level drops suddenly, and if much blood is lost, a visit to the hospital is necessary for a transfusion of packed red cells and oral or intravenous fluids.

Mrs. Virginia White is a sickle cell anemia patient who leads a productive life and has learned to cope with the day-to-day problems of her disease.

As a young girl, in Meridian, Mississippi, Virginia did all the physical things her friends did—jumped rope, climbed trees, and swung on a grapevine over a creek. But when she overexerted herself she paid the price in pain. These pains were called rheumatism by the family doctor who at that time had no knowledge of sickle cell disease.

It was during her high school years that the diagnosis was made. Virginia was an honor student, playing basketball and twirling a baton in the marching band when she came down with what was thought to be a viral infection. In the hospital, after several tests, her illness was diagnosed as sickle cell disease.

What was sickle cell disease? Virginia wanted to know. She read everything she could find on the subject, so that she knew all about her condition.

"I made up my mind not to ever let it get me down," Virginia said, "though I had to tough it out through several crises."

Virginia continued to study hard, play basketball, and lead the marching band. When she went to college, she decided on a career in the legal profession. But after suffering a serious sickle crisis complicated with pneumonia, she was told that the years of schooling required to become a lawyer would be too strenuous for her.

She wouldn't listen. She was determined to be a lawyer. As soon as Virginia recovered she finished her undergraduate work and went on to complete law school.

Virginia White married and had three children; she started a nursery school, and although she didn't have time to study for the bar, she never lost sight of her goal to practice law. Then, when her youngest child was five, Virginia suffered a severe sickle cell crisis. She was depressed to have come so far toward her professional goal only to have it snatched from her by her horrible illness.

It was Virginia's family who gave her the strength to keep going. The two oldest children learned to give her shots for pain and watched to see that she had plenty of liquids at her bedside during a crisis. They took her temperature and helped her telephone the doctor. They baby-sat for their little brother and assisted their father with household chores. Most of all, they gave Virginia their love. The entire family, including the little five-year-old, learned how to deal with sickle cell disease.

Although she had almost given up, Virginia was finally able to return to her nursery school. Following doctor's orders, she worked there part-time, and while resting at home, studied for the bar. It took her a year to get up the courage to take the exam, but she finally did—and passed it the first time. She is now practicing law.

Virginia White's story is an example of what determination and a loving family can do to beat sickle cell disease.

WHAT'S IN THE FUTURE FOR SICKLE CELL ANEMIA PATIENTS?

Today, we are much better informed about sickle cell disease. Patients live longer and the quality of life is improved due to better information, screening, and improved medical care.

Various methods to prevent blood cells from sickling have been tried, but so far no drug has been discovered that will prohibit sickling.

The most progress has been made in the area of screening, and large groups of the general population are now being tested for sickle cell trait.

Great strides have also been made in prenatal testing where researchers are trying to invent new techniques to prevent sickle cell disease. Some of these techniques involve genetic engineering and the search for an antisickling drug.

Researchers are moving closer to replacing the faulty gene that serves as a blueprint for the abnormal protein, hemoglobin S, with a healthy one. When these techniques are perfected, they may become therapy for those with genetic blood disorders like sickle cell disease, and so there is considerable hope for the future.

Chapter Six

TAY-SACHS DISEASE

Cyd, the baby daughter of Todd and Rebecca Gold, was six months old when she was diagnosed as having Tay-Sachs. Rebecca had just read a pamphlet about the disease in the doctor's waiting room, and couldn't believe that her beautiful little girl had the terrible illness.

When they took Cyd out in her stroller and people admired the baby's porcelain complexion and long, black eyelashes, Todd would say, "She's our china doll."

Until Cyd was six months old, she was developing like any other normal child. But then her parents noticed that something was wrong. She stopped crawling and trying to push herself up. Any little noise startled her. If they propped her up on the sofa, she would lean and fall over. They took her to the doctor because they thought she might need physical therapy.

The diagnosis of Tay-Sachs disease was shocking to the Golds. They were told that Cyd's porcelain skin and long lashes were common traits among Tay-Sachs children. And they soon learned that they would have to face the gradual deterioration of their beautiful daughter.

When Cyd was a year old she couldn't hold her head up, and at about sixteen months of age she began to lose her sight. She developed a staring look and went blind. She was no longer able to sit up by herself, crawl, or talk.

Feeding became a problem. Because Cyd couldn't swallow her food, it took Rebecca three to three and a half hours to feed her at each meal. Eventually, because the baby didn't get enough liquids, a tube was inserted into her stomach and she was fed through the tube.

It became too difficult for Todd and Rebecca to handle their child at home, and she was placed in an institution. Little Cyd died in her sleep at the age of four.

WHAT IS TAY-SACHS DISEASE?

Tay-Sachs disease (TSD) is a genetic disorder in young children that causes progressive loss of mental and motor ability. Those who have this rare disease are missing an important enzyme called hexosaminidase A (hex-A), which breaks down fatty materials (lipids) in the brain and central nervous system. Because the fat isn't broken down it builds up in the brain tissue and eventually destroys the brain cells.

The disease process starts early in the fetus of a pregnant woman, but TSD isn't usually diagnosed until several months after birth, when the symptoms begin to show. Even with good care, most TSD children die before they reach the age of five.

TSD was named for Dr. Warren Tay, an ophthalmologist, and Dr. Bernard Sachs, a neurologist. They were the first doctors to identify a degenerative disease of the central nervous system caused by the absence of hex-A.

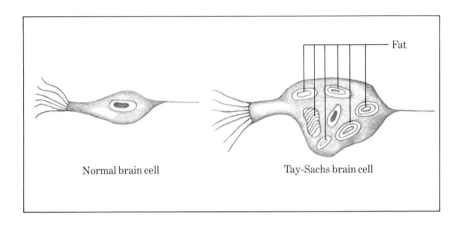

Normal brain cell   Tay-Sachs brain cell

WHAT ARE THE SYMPTOMS OF TAY-SACHS DISEASE?

A baby born with Tay-Sachs disease seems healthy at birth and appears to develop normally, but somewhere between the ages of three to six months there is a change. At first, even the parents may not notice it. Before long, the baby stops crawling, making sounds, playing, and smiling. Soon the stricken infant can't sit up anymore, or roll over, or reach for anything.

From two years on there are chronic respiratory problems. As the disease gets worse, it becomes difficult for the child to eat, and he or she may suffer many coughing spells while eating. Sudden noises can send victims of TSD into fits of screaming.

The regression is slow, and there may be weeks, or even months when it seems that the illness has leveled off. But the child eventually becomes blind, deaf, paralyzed, mentally retarded, and out of touch with reality. Most children die of bronchopneumonia.

HOW IS TAY-SACHS
TRANSMITTED?

This disease, like cystic fibrosis and sickle cell anemia is transmitted by an autosomal (on one of the twenty-three pairs of chromosomes) recessive gene that is passed on from parent to child. It probably began long ago as a mutation in somebody's gene.

Usually, people have a pair of genes that contain the code for production of hex-A. When they become parents, each parent passes one of the genes in the pair to every offspring. If either or both genes are working properly, the body produces hex-A. In a person who is a TSD carrier, one TSD gene is working properly, but the other in the pair (caused by the Tay-Sachs mutation) is not making hex-A. When both parents are carriers, although they are both healthy, their child can inherit one faulty TSD gene from each of them. With a pair of faulty genes, that child will have Tay-Sachs.

A simple blood test can be given to determine a person's hex-A level. The amount of hex-A in the blood tells how many working genes a person has for this important enzyme. A Tay-Sachs baby has no circulating hex-A. A carrier, with one faulty gene and one normal gene, produces about half the normal amount of hex-A. When a carrier is identified, relatives—especially parents—should be tested, so the family can establish a genetic family history.

In prospective parents, if only one person is a carrier their children will not have the disease, but there is a 50 percent chance that each of the children will be a carrier.

If both prospective parents are carriers, as Todd and Rebecca Gold were, they are considered to be at high risk. There is a one-in-four chance (25 percent with each pregnancy) that they will produce a child who will inherit a faulty hex-A gene from each of them and die from Tay-Sachs disease. There is a 50 percent chance with each pregnancy of producing a child who is a carrier and a 25 percent chance that their child will neither be a carrier nor have the disease. Little Cyd Gold, unfortunately, was in the 25 percent) range that inherited a faulty hex-A gene from each of her parents.

POPULATIONS
WITH HIGH RISK

Often genetic diseases occur within certain ethnic groups or geographical locations more frequently than in the general population. We've seen that sickle cell anemia is more common in blacks, and cystic fibrosis is found mostly in whites of Northern European ancestry. Tay-Sachs tends to occur more often in families of Eastern European (Ashkenazi) Jewish origin.

Rebecca and Todd Gold were Jewish, so when Rebecca was pregnant her doctor asked if there was a history of Tay-Sachs in either family. When she said no, he told her that she had nothing to worry about. He should have ordered a blood test to determine whether the Golds were carriers of the Tay-Sachs gene.

Despite the fact that approximately 85 percent of the TSD children are Jewish, and about one in every twenty-five Jews in the United States is a carrier of the TSD gene, Tay-Sachs is not exclusively a Jewish genetic disorder. The disease has been reported among the Amish, Italian Catholics, and in a group of non-Jewish Canadians. The incidence of the disease among non-Jews is about one in three hundred. We don't know exactly how non-Jews who carry the gene inherited it. They may have had Jewish ancestors, or at one time the same or similar mutation that results in the lack of hex-A could have occurred in their ethnic community.

Kim Boyce-Hagerty and her husband, Patrick, had been married for over a year when Beth was born. Beth's sister, Kelly, came along when Beth was not yet two, and that's when Kim and Pat noticed that Beth was changing from the sweet, contented little girl she once was to a cranky child who fell down a lot and didn't talk much. A relative suggested that Beth might have a speech problem. Kim thought Beth just wanted their attention because she was jealous of the baby, but after thinking it over, she took the little girl to the family doctor.

The doctor wasn't worried about the child's speech, but he pointed out that Beth hadn't gained any weight in the last six months and that she had developed an involuntary eye movement. He suggested that Kim take Beth to a pediatric neurologist.

The neurologist found that Beth's brain was not functioning properly. The child was tested for brain tumor, cancer, and numerous other diseases. Finally, the diagnosis was made. Although neither Kim nor Pat were Jewish, their daughter had a rare form of Tay-Sachs disease.

WHAT IS THE TREATMENT FOR TAY-SACHS DISEASE?

At present, there is no treatment for Tay-Sachs disease. An attempt to inject a few patients with hex-A, the missing enzyme, has been tried, but without success. The enzyme didn't go to the brain. Even if it had, we still don't know if it could have reversed the damage already done to the central nervous system, or how much brain damage would remain.

In the early stages of the disease, Kim took Beth to an infant stimulation program and to Shriner's Hospital for occupational therapy to help her daughter keep what motor skills she had. Beth was given nutritional supplements and special skin care. Kim received invaluable advice for feeding Beth from women in a parent group of the National Tay-Sachs and Allied Diseases Association.

When Beth was three, she was taken to a school for the developmentally disabled where she was given range-of-motion exercises to improve her circulation and prevent muscle contractures.

Although Beth's regression was slower than most TSD victims, she eventually lost most of her mental and motor skills. She is almost blind, can no longer feed herself, and can't even say "Mama" anymore. "But in spite of losing these skills," Kim says, "Beth's sweet nature always shows through."

As TSD children regress, they need constant care. The Hagertys cared for Beth at home as long as possible, but when Beth was four, she was placed in a long-term special care facility.

Now Beth is six and a half. She has lived longer than most Tay-Sachs children. It's unusual, too, that she is normal in size and still smiles when the family comes to see her.

SCREENING AND PREVENTION

When TSD appeared in the Gold and Hagerty families, there had been no previous history of the disease in either family. But perhaps long ago in one of the small European towns where their ancestors lived, and where the death of infants and small children was commonplace, some may have died because of Tay-Sachs disease. The TSD gene could have remained hidden for generations and showed up again by chance when two carriers married.

Kim and Pat were tested and found to be carriers of the TSD gene, and although Kim's was the usual TSD genotype, Pat's was a rare kind. Their parents, brothers, and sisters, and even their grandparents were tested. Carriers turned up in both Kim's and Pat's families in four generations. But imagine their relief when their own daughter, Kelly, was found to be TSD free.

The best way we know of to beat this disease is to identify carrier couples and prevent it from happening in the first place. Before carrier testing, the only way to find out if you were a TSD carrier was to become a parent of a TSD baby. It is now possible for couples to find out if they are at risk before they suffer the tragedy of parenting a terminally ill child.

Because Tay-Sachs occurs mostly among the Jewish population, voluntary genetic screening and testing programs began in Jewish communities in 1971. Screening means identifying carriers by measuring the hex-A level in their blood. If results are inconclusive, then white blood cells and tears can be tested to confirm the diagnosis.

Couples planning for a healthy family can have blood samples taken at prevention centers, in hospitals, or at public screenings. When carrier couples are diagnosed, genetic counseling is an important part of the program to help them get over the anxiety of carrying a TSD gene and to tell them of their reproductive options.

Genetic counseling is advisable for all young adult TSD carriers. There is no danger of transmitting the disease if the carrier picks a mate who is not a carrier.

Prospective parents who are TSD carriers and want to know if the baby they are expecting is healthy can have samples of amniotic fluid from the expectant mother diagnosed for hex-A by amniocentesis. This is the method we spoke of in an earlier chapter whereby pregnancies are monitored when genetic or medical problems are suspected. It is usually done in the sixteenth to eighteenth week of pregnancy.

A newer method now being tested to diagnose genetic disease even earlier—chorionic villi sampling—was also detailed in a previous chapter. When Kim Boyce-Hagerty became pregnant again, she had chorionic villi testing after only eight weeks of pregnancy. She says, "I was in a terrible state waiting for the results." But Kim didn't have to wait long. The good news came the very next day. The Hagerty's developing baby was TSD free!

Patrick Junior is now a healthy fourteen-month-old, and his sister Kelly is delighted to have a little brother to play with.

There are a limited number of laboratories experienced in the complicated procedure of Tay-Sachs testing. Test results must be accurate, and there can be no mix-ups. Workers have to know the procedures well so that they can give experienced interpretations of test results—people depend on the results to plan their future.

Since 1969, when the defective TSD enzyme was identified, almost five hundred thousand people worldwide have been tested for carrier status. The Tay-Sachs screening program has called attention to the fact that the disease can be prevented and that testing is available to detect the couples who are at risk. Because these programs have been so successful, they are considered to be good examples of what can be done to prevent hereditary disease.

Chapter Seven

DIABETES

Jodie Elton was a healthy seven-year-old who liked school and especially enjoyed reading, until she came down with a *virus*. After two weeks at home resting, Jodie went back to school, but there was a big change in the second grader. She was tired all the time and couldn't concentrate on her work. Because she had to go to the bathroom so often, the other children made fun of her, so she made up excuses to stay at home.

What was wrong with Jodie? She was always hungry, and although she ate a lot, she was losing weight. She drank plenty of fluids, but she complained of being thirsty all the time. Jodie's mother took her to the doctor for a checkup.

The doctor examined Jodie. Her symptoms pointed to diabetes, but he decided to take tests before he made his diagnosis. The urine test showed the presence of sugar, which is not normal. Jodie's blood test also showed a higher-than-normal amount of sugar. Jodie had Type I diabetes.

In this form of diabetes, the pancreas cannot produce *insulin*, and since insulin is necessary to stay alive, Jodie must take daily insulin *injections*. Insulin, which is a protein, cannot be taken as a pill because the stomach would use it as a protein, like meat, and it would not be used as insulin.

Jodie's doctor worked out a schedule of the amount and type of insulin she would require, and when to take it. He also gave her a meal plan that was a nutritious, well-balanced diet consisting of fruits, vegetables, meat, breads, and milk, eliminating "junk" food and simple sugars. Jodie was happy to know that she didn't have to give up foods she liked such as jello, pudding, or soda as long as they were sugar free. She was told to never skip a meal, to eat whenever she felt hungry, and to eat before gym or other exercise. If Jodie used insulin, and followed her food program, she could go to school, take gym, swim, and bike as she normally did. Her parents learned to give her the insulin shots and helped her to balance her food, insulin, and physical activity.

Everyone in the second grade thought the medical tag that Jodie wore was special. It said: I have diabetes. My name is Jodie Elton. My home telephone number is 948-5555. My doctor is Dr. Egel at Community Hospital.

WHAT IS DIABETES?

Diabetes is a chronic disease for which there is no cure. It affects the way the body uses food and causes sugar levels in the blood to be too high.

Our bodies need food for everything we do, from thinking to playing ball. During digestion, our food is changed into *glucose*. Glucose, a sugar, is the main fuel that the body burns for energy. When glucose begins to circulate in the bloodstream, it needs something to help it enter the body cells to utilize the energy. A hormone called insulin is that substance.

Insulin comes into the bloodstream by attaching itself to a *receptor site* on the cell, therefore allowing the glucose to enter the cell. You might think of insulin as the key that opens the door (receptor site) to allow the glucose or sugar from foods we eat to enter the cell to produce energy. Some glucose enters the blood, the rest is stored in the liver. Glucose is also stored in the muscle for later use.

If you do not have diabetes, insulin works with another hormone named *glucagon* to keep exactly the right amount of sugar in your blood. Insulin is secreted by the beta cells of the pancreas; glucagon is made by the alpha cells. Both the alpha and beta cells are in the islets of Langerhans in the pancreas.

The amount of these hormones that is produced depends on how much sugar is in the blood. When there is more sugar the pancreas secretes or gives out more insulin, and the blood sugar level goes down. If there is not enough sugar, the pancreas makes more glucagon, which makes the blood sugar level go up.

When a person has diabetes, something goes wrong with this important process. Food is changed into glucose, but the pancreas either stops making insulin or doesn't produce enough. Without enough insulin, glucose cannot be used by the body as a source of energy, and there is too much sugar in the blood.

TYPES OF DIABETES

More than seven million people in the United States suffer from diabetes. About five million more have the disease and are unaware of it. It is not contagious, yet it is one of the worst diseases of our time.

Anyone can get diabetes, men as well as women, and people of any age, even babies. Researchers aren't sure if diabetes is one or ten or twenty diseases. Several different types of this disease have been identified so far. The two major kinds are Type I (insulin-dependent) formerly called juvenile diabetes, and Type II (non-insulin-dependent) formerly called maturity-onset diabetes.

Type II is the most common form of diabetes and occurs most often in people over forty. It usually comes on gradually.

When Jodie Elton's father was forty-eight years old, he complained to the doctor that he was always tired, his body ached, and sometimes his toes or fingers felt numb. He was overweight and needed to lose about 25 pounds (11 kg).

After an examination, the doctor found sugar in his urine. It could have been a temporary condition, but since Jodie had diabetes and Mr. Elton was overweight, the doctor asked him to take a blood sugar test the next morning before breakfast.

Mr. Elton's test showed that he had Type II diabetes. In Jodie's case, Type I, her body made no insulin; her father's body made some insulin, but it wasn't working effectively.

The doctor asked Mr. Elton to change his eating habits. He was told to eat fewer starches, no sweets, cut down on fats and fried foods, and include raw vegetables and fresh fruits in his diet. He had to weigh himself weekly, reduce his calories, and exercise daily. Mr. Elton was also taught relaxation techniques to reduce stress.

After a while, because diet and exercise didn't bring down Mr. Elton's blood sugar level enough, the doctor prescribed a pill called an *oral hypoglycemic*. This medication helps the pancreas produce more insulin or improves the way the insulin functions. People with Type I diabetes, like Jodie, can't use pills because their bodies produce no insulin. If Mr. Elton hadn't shown improvement after taking the medicine, he, too, would have required insulin injections to keep his blood sugar normal.

WHAT CAUSED JODIE'S DIABETIC SYMPTOMS?

Because Jodie's body made no insulin, the glucose in her bloodstream couldn't be used by the cells to make energy. Instead, it collected in her blood and led to high sugar levels.

The cells needed glucose, so Jodie felt hungry. Even if she took in extra glucose by eating more, the glucose could not get to the cells or be stored by her body. So, her body had to find other sources of energy, and fat deposits and protein stores were broken down to provide it.

When fat deposits are broken down, acid by-products called *ketone* bodies are released into the blood. Too many ketones can poison cells by making the blood too acidic. This caused Jodie to lose weight and feel weak and tired.

The kidneys try to clear the blood of excess glucose by excretion in the urine. In order to do this, they must dilute the glucose with extra water. Excess water made Jodie go to the bathroom frequently. Sugar in the urine is a sign that blood sugar has been high enough to make the body spill some off into the urine. Moderate to large amounts of ketones in the urine means that the body does not have enough insulin. Jodie was often thirsty because of losing large amounts of water in the urine.

When Jodie had a sore it took a long time to heal. Her doctor said that because her blood contained too much sugar and was too acidic, it interfered with the way her white blood cells fought infection.

DIABETES AND HEREDITY

Although we've learned a great deal in the past ten years about diabetes, the specific cause of Type I diabetes is still a mystery. In a study of the inheritance of diabetes done on identical twins, in which twins were split up into separate groups, it was found that if one identical twin group had Type I diabetes, the other group got it only 46 percent of the time. If one identical twin group had Type II diabetes, however, the other group got it 100 percent of the time. In another study, researchers found that often when a child developed Type I diabetes, there was no one else in the family with the disease. So conclusions were drawn from these studies that Type II diabetes is inherited, but Type I is not.

Although scientists know that genes probably play a major role, they still haven't been able to identify which genes make a person susceptible to Type II diabetes, what processes are involved that turn the potential diabetic into a true one, and how it can be prevented from happening.

It has recently been discovered that children with Type I diabetes have certain proteins on the surface of many body cells that are called HLA antigens. Genes that control the production of HLA antigens have been located on chromosome six. After many studies, scientists decided that other factors must combine with an inherited susceptibility before diabetes will develop, but they aren't sure what they are.

This disease is hard to figure out. Although a family history usually reveals that a blood relative has or had diabetes, what is passed on is the tendency to get the disease, not the disease itself. Children of people with diabetes who do not have the disease may pass the trait on to their offspring.

OTHER CAUSES
OF DIABETES

In Type I diabetes, several kinds of viruses and a process called *autoimmunity* are believed to trigger the disease. Researchers have found a certain antibody in the blood of children with the disease. It attaches itself to the beta cells in the pancreas and works to kill germs in the same way that our immune system does when we catch a cold. In diabetes, it seems that the body's immune system goes awry and mistakenly sees its own cells as a foreign substance. It attacks and tries to destroy them the way a body sometimes rejects a kidney or heart transplant. If this causes diabetes, then what makes the immune system go wrong?

We know that a number of viruses destroy the islet cells in the pancreas. Perhaps viruses that cause childhood diseases attack the insulin-producing beta cells in the same way and cause changes in the body's immune system. We still aren't sure, though, whether the changes in the immune system come before or after the genetic and/or environmental influences.

In type II diabetes, there is risk that older people, those who are obese, and women who have had large babies will get the disease. Diabetes affects these groups more than others possibly because the beta cells of their pancreas have been overworked.

Other factors that trigger a sudden lack of insulin and bring on the symptoms of diabetes could be surgery, enormous shock from severe injury in an accident, or an intense emotional upset, such as a death in the family.

WHAT IS THE TREATMENT FOR DIABETES?

Programs like Jodie's and Mr. Elton's are often set up with a health care team—a nurse-educator, dietitian, exercise specialist, and counselor. Working with the doctor the health care team tries to find a balance of food, insulin, and exercise that will keep the patient's blood sugar levels as close to normal as possible. Patients and their families are then taught self-management skills.

Over the years, Jodie has learned an enormous amount about diabetes in order to accomplish these skills. Now that she is twelve she gives herself insulin injections. She also does blood glucose monitoring in order to determine what the proper amount of insulin is for her. With a simple "finger stick" and a small monitoring machine, such as Accu-Chek II, she gets a specific numeric value. She can see what her blood sugar level is, call the doctor, and readjust her insulin dosage. She does this blood sugar test from two to seven times a day. Jodie has also been educated in matters such as what to eat in restaurants, at parties, and how to manage sick days.

Blood glucose monitoring can also be used by those with Type II diabetes. Even when taking medication or insulin, people with Type II diabetes must stay on their diet and exercise plan.

Before insulin was discovered in 1922, a diagnosis of Type I diabetes was always a death sentence. At first it was thought that insulin was a cure for diabetes. It was not, but it has become a lifesaver for many people.

After years of research, it was found that the hormone from the pancreas of pigs and cattle was similar to that produced by the human body, and it could be used in the treatment of diabetes. Humulin Insulin, a synthetic insulin that is identical to human insulin, is also available now.

Insulin is mixed with other substances that cause the substances to differ in how long they act to lower blood sugar, how quickly they start working, and how soon after the injection they act most strongly. One kind of insulin goes to work immediately and lowers blood sugar for about six hours. Then another injection is needed. Other kinds of insulin take longer to work and last twenty-four hours or more. Sometimes a mixture of these kinds of insulin is used, and the amount and type of insulin is adjusted from time to time.

How does a doctor know how much insulin to give each patient? Until recently there was no reliable way to measure exactly how much insulin a patient's pancreas pumps out each day. Researchers are now testing a new method to measure a patient's insulin needs that they say is at least 90 percent accurate. The new technique will help doctors tell the difference between those who must have insulin injections and others who can manage the disease with pills or diet.

BALANCING SUGAR AND INSULIN

If people with diabetes follow their treatment plan, there shouldn't be any problems. There may be times, however, when too much food is eaten, there is not enough exercise, the insulin dose is not large enough, or the patient is ill or under stress, and a problem will occur because of high blood sugar. This is called *hyperglycemia*.

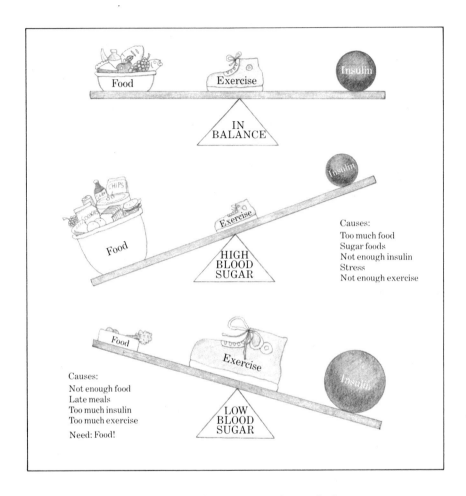

*Balanced blood sugar requires a balance
of food, exercise, and insulin.*

When sugar and insulin are unbalanced, poisonous ketones accumulate in the blood. The condition could lead to diabetic coma (ketoacidosis) and death if it is not corrected immediately.

A person with diabetes can also have problems when there is too much insulin resulting in too little sugar in the blood. It can happen if a person takes too much medication, misses a meal, or performs heavy exercise. This condition is called insulin reaction, or *hypoglycemia*. Because not enough sugar goes to the brain, the brain cells will not work properly, producing symptoms such as hunger, weakness, sweating, unnatural actions, or fuzzy vision. Low blood sugar must be treated promptly with a small amount of sugar—a half glass of orange juice or hard candy. The extra sugar goes into the blood and brings the level back to normal.

DIABETIC COMPLICATIONS

Sometimes medical problems known as complications can occur in people who have had diabetes for a long time. The more sugar in the blood, the higher the chance for deposits of fatty and other materials to build up. In time, this plaque narrows the blood vessels and arteries, making them thicken and clog. This reduces the blood flow and causes damage to the heart, brain, legs, and feet. The small blood vessels of the eye and kidney are also at risk. Diabetes is the leading cause of blindness. But not everyone with diabetes has complications. With good control, complications can be prevented or at least delayed.

RECENT ADVANCES
AND FUTURE RESEARCH?

Self-monitoring of blood glucose and ketones, antidiabetic medications, laser therapy to prevent diabetes-caused blindness, and new insights into diabetic dietary needs are some of the recent advances that are resulting in longer, healthier lives for people with diabetes.

The insulin pump is a recent development in the management of diabetes. It is used for patients whose diabetes is difficult to control (usually called brittle), for diabetics who are physically

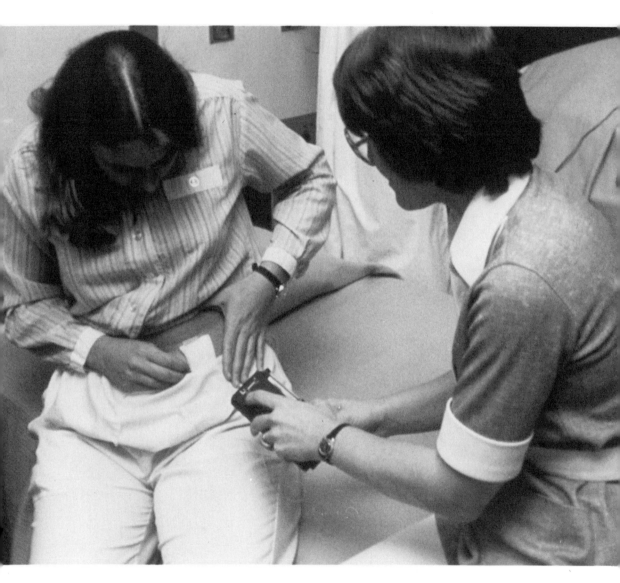

*A nurse shows a diabetic patient
how to use an insulin pump.*

active, and for women who wish to become pregnant and who require perfect control during pregnancy. Today, a pregnant woman with diabetes has a much greater chance of having a normal, healthy baby than she would have had just ten years ago.

Candidates for the pump, after recommendation by their doctors, must be interviewed by a screening team. Once approved, they must be educated to program the pump based on their lifestyle, physical activity, diet, and insulin needs. As small as a deck of cards, the pump injects insulin through a needle into the abdomen. The insulin enters the tissue just beneath the skin and is then absorbed into the bloodstream. The pump is usually worn on a belt or hidden in a pocket. It can be worn for noncontact sports except swimming.

Researchers are also experimenting with pancreas and islet cell transplants. Replacing the damaged tissue might actually allow them to cure diabetes. They are learning how to collect insulin-producing cells, store the tissue, and prevent it from being rejected once transplantation has taken place. It won't be long before major advances are made in this area.

A hormone called somatostatin, found in many tissues including the pancreatic islets, is being investigated. One of the things somatostatin does in the body is to make the pancreas produce less glucagon. An injection of somatostatin may help to bring down the blood sugar level of a person with diabetes.

It's only been a few years since doctors began to unravel the mystery of diabetes. More research is needed to discover how to prevent diabetes and its complications. Scientists are optimistic that a vaccine to prevent the disease in children will be available by the year 2000 or sooner.

Chapter Eight

HOW DO YOU CURE A HEREDITARY DISEASE?

Our ultimate goal is to eliminate hereditary disease. At the present time, however, there are only a few hereditary diseases and disorders, such as cleft lip and cleft palate, that can be completely cured. But due to genetic research, scientists have made some progress in that direction. With injections, new drugs, special diets, and treatments, doctors have been able to help those with hemophilia, diabetes, and several other once-fatal diseases live relatively normal lives.

There has also been progress with screening programs, prenatal testing, and new techniques in prevention of genetic disease. We are getting closer to our goal all the time, but we really don't know yet how to cure most hereditary diseases.

Recently, scientists figured out the complete chemical structure of an organism. This information led to the discovery of how faulty genes upset the cells' biochemistry. The major emphasis now in hereditary disease research is in understanding what is going wrong. If scientists can find the faulty gene or gene product, they will learn what the defect is. In order to do this, they have to be able to read the blueprints of life in their chemical code. When they can, they will use that code to make changes in the existing information molecules, or even to build new ones. Then the body can make its own cure.

Scientists are learning more about genes every day. Recent advances promise that some of their goals are closer to realization now, but there are still many problems to solve.

GENE THERAPY

Rewriting the blueprints in an organism's cells to correct nature's errors, to change and perhaps to improve on nature's design, is called *genetic engineering*. It is through gene therapy that the ultimate goal of genetic engineering can be accomplished.

In gene therapy a copy of a normal gene is inserted into a cell of a patient to do the work that a faulty gene cannot do. This procedure will probably be tried on humans soon, but at present, most of the research has only been done in mice.

HOW WOULD THIS GENE MAGIC WORK ON HUMANS?

Gene therapy began in the 1970s when genetic engineers spliced genes from other organisms into bacteria and created new life-forms. These new genes enabled the bacteria to do valuable work; for example, they could make insulin.

In 1980, when researchers experimented by inserting genes into mice, the results were encouraging. They were able to reverse certain birth defects in their laboratory animals almost entirely, but the mutations that resulted would not have been acceptable to humans.

Scientists believe it is possible to use gene magic on humans, too, because of the DNA molecule, the blueprint of life. Remember that DNA molecules inside the cells determine the hereditary traits of humans as well as other organisms. DNA does this by controlling the formation of the chemical substances or proteins that comprise and regulate the cell. The long DNA molecule has thousands of segments. Each segment or gene is responsible for the formation of a specific protein.

A healthy person has a gene that tells the cell to produce a certain protein. Doctors believe that in patients where that gene is defective, the normal gene can be inserted into their cells and the disease will be cured.

This work involves many carefully planned steps. The first step is to identify the normal gene that is lacking in the victims of hereditary disease, and since every cell has as many as one hundred thousand genes, this is not an easy job. Hundreds of experiments have to be conducted, and doctors must trust to luck a great deal of the time.

When at last they've found the normal gene, copies are made by taking the gene from a healthy cell and inserting it into bacteria or yeast cells. As the cells divide, millions of copies of the normal gene will be produced.

The next step is to deliver these gene copies to the patient's body cells via a natural pest, the virus. A virus is a piece of DNA (or RNA) covered with a membrane, or protein coat. Normally, when a virus invades a cell, it causes infection. The infected cell functions abnormally by taking its orders from the virus's genetic material rather than from its own DNA. Now scientists have learned how to maneuver the viruses so that they deliver the needed genes but do not cause infection in the cell.

The last step in gene therapy is to remove cells from the patient's bone marrow and "infect" them with the virus that carries the normal gene. The treated cells are then put back into the patient's bloodstream where they circulate through the body to the bone marrow. The hope then is that these cells will produce enough of the normal gene to correct the patient's disorder.

(83)

WHAT'S AHEAD

There is still much work to be done in order to prove how well these transplantations will work in human bone marrow cells, how stable and lasting the foreign genes would be in the patient's tissues, and whether these cells would produce enough of the gene's product to cure the disease. About half a dozen American medical teams are presently involved in research and are known to be considering gene therapy on humans.

At first, gene therapy may help only a few hundred or so people who suffer certain rare single-gene disorders. In the coming years, however, this technique could possibly cure many genetic diseases.

The National Institutes of Health has appointed a DNA advisory committee to study gene therapy. Recently the committee issued guidelines for researchers who apply for funds to conduct gene therapy. The committee's approval is needed before there can be experimental treatment in human patients by American scientists.

The committee's guidelines apply only to gene therapy on body cells, such as bone marrow cells. In this therapy the genetic makeup of the patient would be changed, but the changes would not be passed on to the patient's offspring.

Gene therapy on body cells isn't too different from other high-tech treatments such as organ transplants. Some of the problems are the same as those of any other therapy—who should get the treatment and how much it should cost.

It is difficult to guess how soon the first proposal for human gene therapy will come before the DNA advisory committee. The best guess is somewhere from six months to three years.

When gene therapy on body cells becomes an accepted practice, what will be next? Perhaps therapy will be performed in a patient's sperm or egg cell so that the disorder or disease cannot be passed on to the next generation. Scientists must solve many problems, though, before they can attempt even simple sex-cell therapy.

THINK ABOUT THIS

If we can cure cystic fibrosis and sickle cell disease by changing a person's genetic makeup, then what if someone is unhappy about being nearsighted or color blind? Should we cure these "disorders" by gene therapy, too?

Should scientists be allowed to insert genes in humans for what some people consider to be desirable traits, such as tallness or body build? What about gene therapy on embryos? We could, perhaps, produce a race of super people and control our own evolution. Although it's not possible to do these things yet, some say it's only decades away.

Critics of gene therapy think we have already gone too far in trying to change ourselves, and they warn of disaster if genetic engineering is allowed to continue. They say that gene therapy in humans would not be necessary if those at risk for recessive hereditary diseases would have carrier testing before they marry.

Those who criticize genetic engineering also comment that what some people think is a disorder, such as nearsightedness, others don't consider to be one. Who will be the judge, they ask, of what is a disorder and what is not? They fear that gene therapy will get out of control, and they want to stop research now before scientists begin to design people the way engineers design machines.

When critics are reminded of the guidelines that have been set up for future experimentation, they are skeptical. They ask how the guidelines will be implemented and by whom. In the opinion of these critics, guaranteeing good health to all people isn't worth trading for our individuality. Many philosophers agree. They cite the fact that it is precisely because we are all different that life on earth is interesting.

Genetic engineers have been doing difficult research for almost twenty years and have made tremendous advances. They don't agree with the critics. They say they could never design a super race because of the technical obstacles involved. For example, there is no single gene responsible for certain traits some consider desirable—such as musical ability. It would involve a tremendous amount of engineering to manipulate such traits, and it is a hopelessly complicated task.

Scientists say it is important to keep their research going because their goal at present is on disease treatment and prevention. Parents of children with hereditary diseases such as cystic fibrosis, sickle cell anemia, Tay-Sachs, and other diseases beg them to continue their work for the sake of their children who are suffering and dying. These parents want the right to decide for themselves and their children whether to try gene therapy.

There should be discussion right now between philosophers, religious leaders, moralists, and scientists before human gene therapy becomes a reality. Questions must be asked and explanations made by scientists so that the issue is clarified.

If we set up proper guidelines clearly stating agreed-upon limits, and provide for supervision of research, the decision will probably be to continue with experimentation. The possibility of an end to suffering and an improvement in the quality of life for those unlucky people born with hereditary disease could be well worth the ethical risks.

Glossary

Achondroplastic dwarfism: An autosomal dominant disorder which, because of a defective change of cartilage into bone, causes a person with this disease to be considerably smaller than average and in some ways abnormally formed.

Amniocentesis: A surgical procedure whereby a sample of amniotic fluid is obtained through a hollow needle inserted into the uterus of a pregnant woman through the abdominal wall and tested for genetic abnormalities.

Amnion: A fluid–filled bag of tissue where the fetus grows inside the mother.

Autoimmunity: A process in which a person's immune system turns against the body and tries to destroy a portion of it.

Autosomes: 22 of the 23 pairs of chromosomes that appear in cells of males as well as females.

Body blueprint: A plan.

Carrier: A person who carries a hidden or recessive gene.

Cell: The smallest self-contained living unit—building blocks of the body.

Cell reduction: Meiosis.

Character: Trait.

Chorionic villi sampling: A new method of diagnosing genetic disease in the ninth to eleventh week of pregnancy.

Chromosome: Any of the thread–like forms in the nucleus of plant and animal cells that contain units of heredity called genes.

Cystic fibrosis: A hereditary disease of young people that affects primarily the lungs and digestive system.

Diabetes: A chronic disease of insulin deficiency or resistance. Type I—insulin dependent—requiring daily insulin shots. Type II—non-insulin dependent.

Diagnosis: The act or process of identifying or determining the nature of a disease by way of examination.

Down syndrome: A genetic disorder characterized by mental retardation and various physical traits, and due to a person having three chromosomes number 21 instead of two. Also called Trisomy 21.

DNA (deoxyribonucleic acid): The main part of a gene which carries the blueprint or code containing the information that determines heredity and directs the growth of every cell in the body.

Dominant gene: Gene that always expresses its characteristic in the person who has it—it overpowers or excludes a recessive gene.

Electron microscope: Microscope that uses beams of electrons instead of beams of light and has much more power than an ordinary microscope.

Embryo: A developing organism before hatching or birth, such as an unborn child.

Environment: All the factors which surround a thing or an individual which can affect its development.

Enzyme: Any of numerous proteins or joined proteins produced by living organisms and functioning as bio–chemical catalysts in living organisms.

Fertilization: The union of egg and sperm resulting in a cell containing two sets of chromosomes—one set derived from the male and one from the female.

Fetus: An unborn animal in later stages of development—in humans the developing baby is called a fetus from the beginning of the ninth week of pregnancy until birth.

Gametes: Human reproductive cells (sperm and egg) of sexually reproducing organisms containing half of a full complement of the genetic program.

Gene: A segment of the chemical DNA, which carries a basic unit of hereditary information in coded form—determines what characteristics will be passed on from parents to children.

Genetics: The study of heredity—how parents pass on certain characteristics such as skin, hair, or eye color to children.

Genetic code: A system of signals for sending messages—tells each cell what to do and when to do it.

Genetic engineering: Rewriting the blueprints in an organism's cells, to correct nature's errors, to change and perhaps improve nature's design.

Glucagon: A hormone produced in the pancreas. Can be given as a shot to raise the blood sugar during a serious insulin reaction.

Glucose: A form of sugar (from food that is eaten) that is a fuel for the cell which changes it into energy.

Heredity: The passing of characteristics from parents to their children.

Hemoglobin: A protein found in red blood cells.

Hemophilia: A hereditary plasma-coagulation disorder mostly affecting males, but transmitted by females and marked by excessive, sometimes spontaneous bleeding.

Hormone: A substance produced by a gland. Hormones help the body to work normally.

Hyperglycemia: High amount of sugar in blood.

Hypoglycemia: Insulin reaction—too little sugar in the blood.

Identical twins: Twins that develop from the same egg.

Injection: Introducing a fluid into the skin, muscle or blood vessels, or body cavity with a medical instrument.

Insulin: A hormone produced by the pancreas. Insulin helps sugar to get into each cell, where it can be changed into energy. Everyone needs insulin to stay alive.

Karyotype: A chromosome study to determine if there are abnormalities.

Ketones: The waste product in the body when there is not enough insulin.

Membrane: A thin, pliable layer of tissue covering surfaces or separating or connecting regions, structures, or organs of plants and animals.

Mendel's laws: Laws discovered by Gregor Mendel describing the inheritance of characters in plants and animals.

Meiosis: Reduction of chromosomes during cell division in gametes by one-half.

Mitosis: Cell division.

Molecule: The smallest unit into which a substance can be divided and still keep its original structure.

Multifactorial inheritance: Diseases that result from at least two inherited abnormal genes interacting with environmental factors.

Mutagens: Substances that bring about chemical changes in the cell and cause a breakdown in the normal structure of a gene or a group of genes.

Mutation: A change in a gene or chromosome that can be inherited.

Nondisjunction: Improper chromosome separation.

Nucleus: A central structure in the cell that controls the cell's activities—a part of the cell in which lie all the materials that are used for reproduction.

Oral hypoglycemic: Pill taken orally by people with diabetes to help the pancreas produce more insulin.

Ovum: A female egg cell.

Pancreas: A long, soft, irregularly-shaped gland located behind the stomach, that secrets digestive juices and produces insulin.

Pregnant: The state of containing an unborn child within the body.

RNA (ribonucleic acid): General name for three substances that act as messengers which deliver the genetic code to the cells and see that the messages are carried out.

Radiation: The act of giving out radioactive materials that can cause damage to the genes and chromosomes.

Receptor site: Place on the cell which allows glucose or sugar from foods we eat to enter the cell.

Recessive gene: A gene that does not express itself when paired with a dominant partner, but will express itself if paired with a like gene.

Reduction division: Meiosis.

Sickle-cell anemia: A hereditary disease in which some of the red blood cells have an abnormal form of hemoglobin and may collapse to a sickle shape, clumping together and clogging blood vessels.

Species: A group of animals or plants that have certain permanent characteristics in common, such as the human species—each species has its own blueprint in its DNA and can breed together to produce fertile offspring.

Sperm: A male reproductive cell.

Tay-Sachs disease: A hereditary degenerative disease in young children that causes progressive loss of mental and motor ability.

Trait: Character or characteristic.

Translocation: Abnormal chromosome change.

Trisomy 21: Down's syndrome.

Virus: A minute germ that can cause an infection or disease because it reproduces inside cells of other organisms.

X-linked or sex-linked: Recessive condition—a hereditary trait that is transmitted by a gene on one of the sex chromosomes and therefore is found mainly in one sex.

X-ray: A form of radiation often used for diagnostic purposes.

Zygote: A fertilized egg—cell formed by union of a sperm and ovum.

For More Information

Arnold, Caroline. *Genetics: From Mendel to Gene Splicing*. New York: Franklin Watts, 1986.

Asimov, Isaac. *How Did We Find Out about Our Genes?* New York: Walker and Company, 1983.

Bornstein, Sandy, and Bornstein, Jerry. *New Frontiers in Genetics*. New York: Julian Messner, 1984.

Dacquino, V. T. *Kiss the Candy Days Good-Bye*. New York: Delacorte, 1982.

Fichter, George S. *Cells*. New York: Franklin Watts, 1986.

Roy, Ron. *Where's My Buddy?* New York: Apple Paperbacks-Scholastic, 1983.

Information on some of the diseases discussed in this book is also available from the following foundations:

American Diabetes Association
National Headquarters
2 Park Avenue
New York, NY 10016

Cystic Fibrosis Foundation
6000 Executive Boulevard
Rockville, MD 20850

Juvenile Diabetes Foundation International
60 Madison Avenue
New York, NY 10010-1550

Midwest Association for Sickle Cell Anemia
36 South Wabash Avenue, Suite 1113
Chicago, IL 60603

National Association for Sickle Cell Disease, Inc.
3460 Wilshire Boulevard, Suite 1012
Los Angeles, CA 90010-2273

National Tay-Sachs and Allied Diseases Association
92 Washington Avenue
Cedarhurst, NY 11516

Index